The Psychology of a Patriot

Praise for the Book

What is patriotism and why is it given so much importance in today's politics? That is the question generations of Indians born after 1947 have tried to grapple with and comprehend as we are faced with much graver problems of climate change, pandemics, poverty and the rise of warring ideologies. Saket Suman tries to find an answer here, and posits the question within the larger context of what humankind seeks today. For itself, and for its future generations.

—**Pritish Nandy**, Veteran editor and Former MP

Saket Suman has been an impassioned commentator on the arts and society. His new book *The Psychology of a Patriot* traces the socio-political history of India through the eyes of three protagonists: Arundhati Roy, Narendra Modi and Shashi Tharoor. A vital argument about the very essence of patriotism and its consequences has been awakened in the Indian Polity.

—**Sanjoy Roy**, Producer of Jaipur Literature Festival and
Managing Director at Teamwork Arts

In *The Psychology of a Patriot*, Saket Suman traces the meaning of patriotism through a readable, often anecdotal account of India's recent history, charting its double-edged power: a force that inspired the Independence struggle, and yet has been misused to foment intolerance and disunity. As a journalist who has written the 'first draft' of the recent history, Suman artfully uses the lives of some Indians, from Romila Thapar to Arundhati Roy and even myself, to delineate his vision of patriotism. Timely and important.

—**Shashi Tharoor**, Noted author, MP and Former Under
Secretary-General of the United Nations

The Psychology of a Patriot

SAKET SUMAN

RUPA

Published by
Rupa Publications India Pvt. Ltd 2021
7/16, Ansari Road, Daryaganj
New Delhi 110002

Sales centres:
Allahabad Bengaluru Chennai
Hyderabad Jaipur Kathmandu
Kolkata Mumbai

ISBN: 978-93-91256-39-5

First impression 2021

10 9 8 7 6 5 4 3 2 1

The moral right of the author has been asserted.

Printed at Parksons Graphics Pvt. Ltd, Mumbai

In memory of fallen Indians who lost their lives in the pandemic because we had put our collective patriotism to rest.

∾

Contents

Preface

When we outlive our time in the womb, where Mother Goddess nurtures us with her many bounties, we make our way out of her body and acquire the distinct traits and features of a complete individual for the first time. This surreal occasion marks the beginning of a new human life. Animals, birds and marine creatures are also blessed with the grace of motherhood—an intimate and extremely intense process of upbringing that culminates in the revival of a similar cycle that goes on from one generation to the next.

But then the most symbolic aspects are passed on to us and we are expected to carry them forward, even if it means doing so blindly. It is regarded as an absolute necessity to obey the path carved out by our forefathers and to consider it as our shared destiny. Nations, castes and religions are thus stamped on to our identities soon after our birth. This happens with very little of our understanding or participation. It does not matter whether we seek pride and honour in these identities or whether we are ashamed and humiliated by the atrocities involved in keeping these systems running because, frankly, we are far too young to make sense of these complicated things that govern our imagination when they become part and parcel of our lives. Our upbringing is then marked by a constant process of getting accustomed to the rules and rituals that our families hold dear and adhere to. As years roll by and as the innocence of the child gets marred by worldly wisdom, the affection that one shares with one's mother finds resonance in that which we fondly and, sometimes passionately, call the motherland.

But was it always the case?

Perhaps no, because we have made discoveries and findings, which travel back into the annals of history to trace the origin of the planet we call home and the stages it traversed to acquire its current shape.

While we are still not quite sure that the earth is the only planet that supports life, we do know, by virtue of logic and common sense, that life on earth emerged after our planet came into being. And after life, came humans, tribes, civilizations, castes, nations and states. Humans were nomads before they began to settle down in places where they built their homes. Then they began to occupy, cultivate and colonize lands and became civilized.

As these evolutions and migrations took place, our view of the patria, which essentially means 'home', began to be fragmented by narrow domestic walls,[1] though it also helped secure our survival through the dark ages. Survival of the fittest, they said, and humans became masters of the world. As nations were born, patriotism became the pivot around which the entire

---

[1]Rabindranath Tagore, *Gitanjali*. India: Rupa & Company, 2002.

system of societal governance began to be constructed. Etching borders and boundaries over the bare body of our planet, our quest to command dominance led to the formation of powerful and powerless nations, thereby heralding an endless conflict on the face of earth. This subsequently resulted in the celebration of valour, courage and sacrifice for the protection and interests of the motherland, and those who dedicated themselves to the cause of their countries came to be known as patriots. The ancestral lineage among the communities that became instrumental in the formation of nations meant that generation after generation would live in the warp of their nationality. We humans have perpetually been trapped inside our heads. Our beliefs and understandings about the world are limited by our ignorance and we have become prisoners of our own imagination as these identities are prone to getting misconstrued and exaggerated over time.

Being a patriot does not, and it never did, necessarily mean caring for the planet in the logical scheme of things. Patriotism denotes one's attachment towards the patria, which is vaguely regarded as one's country and it is in its interests that one is required to live one's life as a citizen. The country, however, is a very recent phenomenon in the total span of the earth. And still, most of us find a sense of comfort in the patria. It is on this promise that we have come thus far, we say to ourselves, and in its guidance shall we march onward.

Understanding patriotism is not easy. It seems familiar because we have heard of it, or seen it manifest itself on numerous occasions. Patriotism, for most, is a sense of attachment towards a homeland. It is something we live with, an almost inseparable part of the national identities that we adhere to. It can, as it usually does, turn dormant for a prolonged period of time, but several political uprisings have since relied, partly or wholly, on patriotism for absorbing, retaining or remaining in power. It has, on the other hand, also been the premise on which the struggles for freedom—from colonialism, dictatorship or monarchy—have been built in several cases.

It is, therefore, not surprising that to openly call one unpatriotic is almost criminal in many countries, while some of the foremost patriots are also seen as hardliners by the intelligentsia and creative practitioners. In other words, patriotism is not necessarily the natural inclination of all, though there is no dearth of those who would want to be identified as patriots too.

The world is at a tipping point as we march into the new decade. Instead of accountability, securities and liberties, people increasingly have to deal with taxes, restrictions and surveillance. And then there are larger challenges, such as climate change and melting glaciers, the outbreak of severe pandemics, violation of human rights, the suppression of liberties and the presence of stark inequalities—all of which are common among nations, though each of them face these in varying measures. There are also different ways in which different people and countries express what patriotism is. While some make a show of it by ridiculing others, others deal with it in a more calm and composed manner.

Many modern nations have been built on the premise of democracy and, in several cases, these have come after bloody wars and massive agitations. While these highlight mankind's innate desire to rule over the rest, they also testify their willingness to strive together. Indians, for example, came to be driven by patriotism during the freedom struggle because they truly hoped and believed that the coming of Independence would result in the end of suffering, suppression, poverty and marginalization by placing the power in the hands of the people. That was the understanding of patriotism during the freedom struggle, which made the coming of Independence such a glorious moment in the history of Indian civilization.

As millions of Indians have been rendered hostile and are pitted against one another, patriotism has almost come to be taken for granted. A very superficial and outward idea of patriotism has been introduced into our lives and implanted in our brains. Waving of flags and chanting of anthems, remaining oblivious to changing times and making superficial gestures are how patriots are defined now. As citizens, we are obliged to pay taxes and discharge our duties. But guarantee of rights and liberties are seldom realized in return, when in fact, patriotism denotes harmony between people and the patria as opposed to a situation where they tolerate, exploit or forsake each other. Patriotism is the solemn manifestation of the bond people share with the patria.

We should be mindful that patriotism can be, and has historically been, manipulated by political and vested interest groups, governments and the powers that be. It should be emphasized that patriotism is neither an isolated sentiment nor is it the only aspect on which the cycle of any given nation or its people revolve, though it is essential in ensuring its safety, security and sovereignty. The arrival of the internet has changed the scheme of things by levelling the playing field, or so we thought, until the bots, troll armies and manipulations came along. So, we need to truly examine the notions that have shaped our understanding of the world we live in. We need to make sense of how patriotism is impacting the collective future of the human race.

Patriotism, to remember, can be a noble idea. Though we quite interpret it as the bond between citizens and the country, we should also not be oblivious to the possibility that somewhere down the line, it can perhaps acquire its larger connotation— that the planet is home and the sense of belonging towards the planet is the supreme form of patriotism.

1

Bharat Bhagya Vidhata

There has been a shared cultural and spiritual temperament that has flourished along the Indian subcontinent since millennia. The Indian civilization has arguably retained its sense of continuity since time immemorial and many Indians take pride in being the flagbearers of the largest continuous civilization that has etched a permanent place in the collective memory of mankind through its rich cultural, spiritual and historical legacy. For the rest of the world too, India has been a very distinct country with peculiar aspects that are not found elsewhere. It is revered to be the country that leads the world and shows the path of Dharma to mankind, to love, to guide and to embrace people of all religions and sects, the Indian nation surely has much to boast and be proud of. There is nothing singular about our country, but we are still one in spirit, in the vibe that makes us Indians. From our varied landscapes to religions and languages, there is a profound sense of richness in the Indian culture that has been documented by renowned writers and philosophers from around the globe.

However, when we trace the origin of the word 'patriotism', we find that it is not very ancient. It is a fairly young word, though its etymological root, patria, which means 'one's native country' or 'homeland', is relatively older and was perhaps first used by ancient Romans to refer to the city. Patria stood for Rome and signified political and societal ethos that Romans were expected to adhere to. It was here that the word acquired its full meaning as it glorified masculinity and conquest while demanding heroism from the Romans. Thus, Brutus says in *Julius Caesar*, 'Not that I loved Caesar less, but that I loved Rome more'. The patria was regarded as sacred and demanded unwavering loyalty from the Romans.

There are two things that patriotism is inherently different from, though it is routinely, sometimes deliberately, confused to mean the same:

1. Patriotism is often defined, or understood, on the same lines as nationalism, but they are two entirely different concepts—similarities and contrasts, though, they may share. George Orwell described patriotism as devotion to 'a particular place and a particular way of life'[1]. The *1984* author specifically distinguished it from nationalism and maintained that patriotism is 'of its nature defensive, both militarily and culturally'.

2. Religion and patriotism do not go well together. The rise

---

[1]Notes on Nationalism, The Orwell Foundation, https://www. orwellfoundation.com/the-orwell-foundation/orwell/essays-and-other-works/ notes-on-nationalism/, accessed 7 May 2021.

of Christianity posed a threat to the concept of patria. For Christians, the geographical territory had little relevance as they identified themselves as members of a shared community. They may have been living in Athens or Rome but taught as they were by their religious leaders to hold their religion above the geographical entity, they found more reason in singing praises of Jesus Christ than surrendering one's devotion to the patria. Mary G. Dietz, the John Evans Professor of political theory at Northwestern University, who has researched extensively on the history of the word 'patriotism', has observed that Christianity threatened to eliminate the political sensibility of patria completely from Rome as worldly territory had minimal relevance for the Christians' understanding of themselves as members of a shared community.[2]

Let us now come to the story of India's independence, traced back to the 1857 revolt, which came to be known as the First War of Independence. It changed the scale and magnitude of things by giving a common objective to Indians. Patriotism, though not unknown, remained largely dormant or fragmented before that because different groups, in the forms of kingdoms and princely states, fought separate battles, just as much among themselves as they did against the foreign aggressors. However, it should also be emphasized that the sense of Indianness and the shared cultural trajectory of the region predated the Sepoy Mutiny too.

---

[2]M.G. Dietz, 'Patriotism,' in Igor Primoratz (Ed.), *Reprinted in Patriotism*, New York: Humanity Books, 2002.

In the absence of democracy, life in the Indian subcontinent is largely said to revolve around spirituality but was there really a religious divide in what was then undivided India? To plainly say no and dismiss all assertions on this front would be inappropriate as religious conversions and interferences with the prevailing Hindu traditions were the hallmarks of several Muslim emperors, though there were also a handful of them who sought to undo it, or at least promote harmony, among the communities. It is also hotly debated that the fostering of Islam in India was made possible because of the pains that were inflicted on the Hindus. Wilful destruction of temples[3] and the imposition of deliberate and targeted taxes on Hindus for practising their religious beliefs were among other sinister designs by which dominance over this region was attained by a series of dynasties.

These historical struggles for dominance seem to have evolved drastically or completely changed their avatar by the year 1857. The very fact that the First War of Indian Independence was fought under the banner of the Mughal emperor Bahadur Shah Zafar[4] makes it clear that religious divide in India had been overcome by the desire of Indians to be free from the shackles of the British Raj. A sense of unity among those who

---

[3]Dhananjay Mahapatra/TNN, 'Who will stop historical wrongs from repeating itself?' *The Times of India*, 1 November 2020, https://timesofindia.indiatimes.com/india/who-will-stop-historical-wrongs-from-repeating-itself/articleshow/78986002.cms, accessed 7 May 2021.

[4]IANS, 'Delhi must hold on to its cosmopolitan culture: Writer Rana Safvi,' *Business Standard*, 10 June 2018, https://www.business-standard.com/article/news-ians/delhi-must-hold-on-to-its-cosmopolitan-culture-writer-rana-safvi-118061000220_1.html, accessed 7 May 2021.

were enslaved by the British had come to thaw the differences they shared among them, though it must have also been very difficult to do away with the painful memories of the past.

We should remember that these were times when the Taj Mahal and other Mughal monuments had already been built. By the 1850s, India was becoming increasingly westernized and the native communities were largely opposed to it. They said that they found their religious beliefs being challenged as missionaries gained a firm footing and began their participation in day-to-day lives. Measures such as common seats for all in the railways were also seen as an interference with the existing religious, societal and cultural disparities among the communities.

While for dynasties, the struggle for dominance moved mostly along religious lines, the fight against the British was different in the sense that Rani Laxmibai of Jhansi and Nana Saheb fought under the Mughal banner[5] instead of that of the Peshwas. The 1857 Hindu-Muslim unity was the first major blow to the British empire. Indians were colonized under *the anarchy* of the East India Company, which, among other things, sought to alter the dynamics that defined the cultural and social ethos of the region. If economic exploitation was a prominent ambition, alteration with the rich cultural heritage of the region also found expression in due course of time. Patriotism in India was born of a deep anger against the the British (or Angrez as

---

[5]Shamsul Islam, 'India's first war of Independence, and the legacy of Hindu-Muslim unity,' *The Indian Express*, 12 May 2020, https://indianexpress.com/article/opinion/columns/1857-india-war-of-independence-hindu-muslim-6405053/, accessed 16 June 2021.

they were called), and people who were infuriated belonged to different faiths.

The suppression by the East India Company had done incalculable damage to the life of the native population, but one of the prominent reasons for the revolt was also the gradual replacement of the old aristocracy with British officials that led to new policies and various introductions which were profoundly opposed to the prevailing customs and rituals. The introduction of something as horrendous as the Doctrine of Lapse by Lord Dalhousie in the late 1840s, for example, had sought to prohibit the Hindu rulers without any natural heirs from adopting their successors, and, not surprisingly, caused widespread resentment among the Hindu rulers as well as their subjects. There was also a sense of growing disenchantment among the zamindari community, as many of its members had lost their lands or the lucrative positions that they enjoyed earlier.

The final spark came in the form of the introduction of the Enfield P53 rifle, which used paper cartridges that came pre-greased. Sepoys were required to bite the cartridge open in order to release the powder while loading the rifle. The grease, however, was said to have included tallow derived from beef and pork, which were offensive to both Hindus and Muslims, respectively. It should also be noted that there were over 3 lakh sepoys and only 50,000 British soldiers. Therefore, the uprising came into being as a concerted effort in several parts of northern and central India. But the rebellion was crushed brutally and, more than anything else, it was the disunity among Indians that led to its failure. Julain Spilsbury noted in *The Indian Mutiny* that the rebellion was put down with the help of other Indian soldiers drawn from the Madras Army, the Bombay Army and the Sikh regiments and that 80 per cent of the East India Company forces were Indian.[6] Several rulers of the princely states were also fighting among themselves and they sided with the British rather than uniting among themselves.

As history goes, the East India Company lost its dominance and India was brought under the direct rule of the British government. Several steps were taken to control future revolts as the British policy became more stringent in the following years. The enthusiastic light-year speed with which patriotism was born in India seemed to have been crushed while Indians were destined to live under foreign occupation, at least for several more decades.

It must be interjected here that many people often consider patriotism and nationalism as the same thing, but the two are different, and the primary difference between them lies in the question of loyalty. It is often seen that staunch nationalists surrender all their loyalty to the idea of nationalism, whereas patriotism rests with the people. The fundamental characteristic of patriotism is that it allows people to be patriotic towards the patria in a manner that the power rests with them. It does not even bind upon people to exhibit their patriotism. Their sense of goodwill towards the patria is subjective and finds utterance as per their will. In the making of the Indian freedom struggle, the desire of the people to be freed from the clutches of British imperialism had a far greater influence than the sense of a Hindu identity of the nation though its reinvigoration was also instrumental in the building up of the freedom struggle. Those

---

[6]Julian Spilsbury, *The Indian Mutiny*, Orion Publishing Group, 2008.

involved in the movement truly believed that the nation that would be born after Independence would regard the will of the people as supreme.

About three decades after India's First War of Independence, a political force was born in the form of the Indian National Congress. The year was 1885 and its founder was A.O. Hume, a retired British officer. Democracy as a principle, or idea or thought, began to emerge slowly as tyranny under the empire became more and more repressive. That people had to find a way to have their say was being strongly felt and an organized political movement as opposed to an armed rebellion now came to challenge the atrocities of the British empire.

Though turbulent and among the darkest of the era of darkness in the subcontinent, the First War of Indian Independence had sparked the spirits of many Indians, and the foundation of the Indian National Congress paved the way for an organized opposition to the British. But patriots were of all kinds—believers and non-believers, preachers of peace and even revolutionaries, the bravehearts as well as the fakirs. Quite interestingly, the party that was founded in 1885 failed to satisfy a large section of those who identified themselves as patriots and who were categorically opposed to the British.

In fact, the Indian National Congress began to lose its popularity barely a decade after it was formed. The reason perhaps was that the Congress, in its early years, was overly moderate in its approach, which resulted in the consolidation of radical ideology towards the beginning of the nineteenth century. It believed in the policy of 'prayer and petition' in its formative years even though its moderate approaches were increasingly proving to be futile. Some leading Congress leaders of those times, such as Surendranath Banerjee, seemed more than impressed by the British sense of justice and, therefore, sought to highlight the concerns and grievances of Indians in manners that were polite and submissive.

On the other hand, despite the 1857 rebellion being crushed brutally, Indians understood one thing: that the British could be defeated if Indians united among themselves in their fight for freedom. The British thrived with their policy of divide and rule, but unity among those they sought to divide could shatter their prospects, and as more and more Indians began to realize this, a militant and revolutionary mood came to grip the hinterlands. Magazines and journals such as the *Kesari* and *Kal* became critical of the Congress's moderate approach and gradually set the ground for the rise of radical patriotism that would rule the roost for the next two decades or so.

Contrary to literal interpretation, the militant mood or the radical patriotism of the time was not necessarily violent in its form, although violence was used by many revolutionaries of the time. For instance, the poetry and other works of provocative literature did not call for radical approaches directly but aroused a sense of pride for the motherland, and thereby, fuelled the rising wave of patriotism in India. The trio of Bal Gangadhar Tilak, Bipin Chandra Pal and Lala Lajpat Rai, on the contrary, opposed the moderate approach, which was also the then policy of the Congress, and popularized slogans such as 'Swaraj is my birthright and I shall have it' at numerous public gatherings. These were parts of their attempts to evoke what they identified as patriotism lying dormant in the hearts of their countrymen.

This fight for swaraj was an outcome of the rising tide of patriotism and its attainment demanded the unity of the people and the awakening of the sense of Indianness. Boycotting foreign goods and passive resistance became tokens of patriotism even though these were not in line with the principles of the Congress party at that time. Bipin Chandra Pal even made it clear that the attainment of swaraj demanded sacrifice and suggested that patriots should be prepared to go to any extent, even if it meant a clash with the authorities. The stories and memories of the First War of Independence served to boost their morale just as rebels such as Kunwar Singh and Mangal Pandey emerged as heroes and icons among the patriots.

The feeling of love for India's glorious past as well as the invocation of its cultural and religious traditions by the likes of Sister Nivedita, Swami Vivekananda, Annie Besant and Swami Dayanand Saraswati helped in the realization of a shared cultural heritage among the people. The literature of that time helped too, as much of it was written as a part of the larger discourse that was taking place in the subcontinent. 'Vande Mataram', which continues to evoke a sense of national pride among Indians even today, had already begun to gain popularity among the masses.

That the economic exploitation by the British was responsible for the plight of Indians was also pointed out. Dadabhai Naoroji, fondly remembered as the 'Grand Old Man of India', pointed to the terrible famines and the bubonic plague in *Poverty and un-British Rule in India*[7]. The culmination of the radical mood in the country helped strengthen the rising wave of patriotism in the subcontinent, but the British fought back with their policy of divide and rule.

---

[7]Dadabhai Naoroji, *Poverty and Un-British Rule in India*, Publications Division, 2016.

The partition of Bengal was aimed at stopping this tide. Lord Curzon, the then viceroy of India, said: 'Bengal united is a power. Bengal divided will pull in several different ways. That is perfectly true and is one of the merits of the scheme.'

But his divisive policy ended up strengthening the morale of radical patriots as massive protests that followed prepared the grounds for a united fight for independence in the long run. *'Amar Sonar Bangla'*, the national anthem of Bangladesh and a popular Bengali song, was composed by Rabindranath Tagore, especially for the protest against the partition of Bengal. Patriotism had become the mood of the region. Even as revolutionaries and freedom fighters were leading the call for freedom and spreading their message among the masses, there were also those who sensed the significance of *Atma Shakti* or self-reliance. A number of industries, such as the Calcutta Potteries and Mohini Mill, were specifically set up to provide employment to native workers so that swadeshi products could be manufactured and British goods could be boycotted. Patriotism, during those days, was not just an idea, but a call to action that would lead towards swaraj.

The swadeshi movement was not successful because the iron-fist handling of the protests by the British broke the morale of the common people. The slogan 'Vande Mataram' was banned and Gurkha soldiers were deployed to curb protests. Those who took part in the movement were expelled from their colleges and disqualified from government services. In response, many patriots used violence against violence. Sacrifice became a celebration.

The British policy of divide and rule sustained even as people struggled to stake their claim over the patria. That *poorna swaraj* (complete independence) should mean the establishment of a Hindu supremacist state was soon demanded by some, but it stood against the principle of unity in diversity, on which the struggle against the British had to be built to defeat the policy of divide and rule. Patriots had been born, but they were still struggling to define what patriotism would mean to them and how it would apply in their daily lives. People were once again as much against the British as they were against those who they thought were not like them, the societal differences began to emerge as reasons behind divisions. The wave of patriotism was being built on the premise of violence. There were many to disagree, but very few to agree with.

2

To Be Worthy of Him

Mahatma Gandhi had hardly been involved with the Indian freedom movement in his early years. Gandhi believed that to achieve freedom, Indians first needed to free themselves from the fear of the British and once this fear was wiped out from their hearts and souls, only then could a struggle for freedom be organized. Hindus and Muslims, in particular, needed to leave behind the burden of the past and unite among themselves to overthrow the empire. 'They cannot take away our self-respect,' he said, 'if we do not give it to them.'

Between 1893 and 1914, the early years that had been among the most turbulent for the Indian National Congress, Gandhi had lived in South Africa and tested the method he would apply in India, though his journey would be entirely different and equally revealing here. Indians living in South Africa faced racial discrimination and were subjected to various indignities, in response to which he led the satyagraha. His fight, he said, would essentially result in the victory of good over evil. He described satyagraha as a weapon of the strongest and stressed that it excluded any form of violence.

India wasn't even independent at that time, but far away in South Africa, Gandhi had united the Indian community and made his fight pro-people, as opposed to anti-empire. That he made the people a stakeholder in the battle is the pivot around which patriotism would revolve in the coming decades. Gandhi's battles were long, but their results are still visible. He understood that patriotism could unite people just as easily as it could tear them apart. Patriotism was vulnerable and Gandhi wanted to ensure that its vulnerability is not exploited, which is why he consistently disagreed with the use of violence in the name of patriotism.

Upon his return to India, Gandhi fought largely for the rights of farmers to protect them from injustice. But he wanted to make the people a stakeholder in the fight and they joined him too. In Champaran in Bihar, farmers joined him in a massive protest as early as 1917. The peaceful yet powerful methods such as Jail Bharo Andolan gradually came to be adopted by those he fought for.

Though patriots in popular media are generally portrayed as violent heroes who lead their countrymen in battles against aggressors and invaders, we often tend to forget that the rise of patriotism is not about individuals but rather about the masses. And Gandhi made it a reality in India.

In fact, more Indians began to identify themselves as patriots under Gandhi's leadership of the Indian National Congress. The fight for freedom gradually became a nationwide movement and people, regardless of their religion, caste or creed wanted to do something that could help in securing freedom because they truly believed that the British were the prime reason behind their suffering. The fight for freedom under Gandhi's leadership was also being built on the promise of democracy, and therefore, people were able to understand that their united power would not only unseat the British empire in India but also help establish a people's government that would work for their collective well-being and upliftment. Gandhi believed in opposing the brutality of the British without violence and, more importantly, without the fear of the British capturing, torturing, imprisoning or killing them. He gave people the confidence to fight for their rights in their agrarian struggles. While the rising tide of radical patriotism in India was thwarted time and again, Gandhi set out on a tiring journey of uniting the larger masses of the country and then leading an organized satyagraha for its independence.

The events that were now going to play out in the Indian subcontinent were quite unprecedented in their magnitude because never had the British imagined that a half-naked fakir would ignite the call for India's freedom in the strongest possible way, and what was till now a sporadic rebellion would become a mass movement against the empire. That this battle was fought with 'satya, dharma and ahimsa' as its core principles were more puzzling still.

There were huge contradictions too. Consider the events leading up to and following the Jallianwala Bagh massacre, for example. A defiant but peaceful crowd had gathered at Jallianwala Bagh on 13 April 1919 when the infamous General Reginald Dyer mercilessly ordered his troops to open fire on the unarmed crowd. It was an act that was equivalent to genocide. And then Gandhi made what he described as the 'Himalayan miscalculation' and launched a satyagraha in its protest. A wave of anger spread through the length and breadth of the country as the news of the massacre spread. To protest against the barbarous act of the British government, Tagore renounced his knighthood, while Gandhi suggested an alternative of fighting the British without violence when they were openly firing on unarmed crowds. The movement was called off and Gandhi himself acknowledged that the people were insufficiently prepared for the discipline that satyagraha demanded.

A genocide such as this was met with a miscalculated response by the Congress as well as Gandhi whereas a radical response to it surfaced two decades later when Udham Singh shot General Dyer at Caxton Hall in London to avenge the massacre of Amritsar. But merely killing Dyer could not have been the solution because as long as the empire thrived, there would be no dearth of merciless British generals and officers as Dyer. Suppression was at the heart of British imperialism and Gandhi wanted to remove the disease as opposed to targeting symptoms.

Patriots are always looking for inspiration and it was not very different during Gandhi's time too. People need heroes, icons and idols to look up to and admire. Gandhi became that figure among the masses. Millions of Indians came to be inspired by his leadership and joined the national movement, dedicating their lives to the cause of independence and remaining undeterred by fears of imprisonment or other British tactics of repression. And yet Gandhi's belief in his principles was so strong that he would not hesitate to withdraw an entire movement, brewed with much effort and sacrifice, the very moment it went against his principles. During those days, being patriotic in India could almost be equated with following Gandhian principles and his methods of struggle.

Satyagraha gradually became the symbol of rebellion in India. Opposing the British and fighting for their rights became tokens of nationalism just as adherence to morals and principles of dharma became the founding pillars of India's freedom movement. The half-naked fakir enabled Indians to look into the eyes of their imperialists and tell them that they were wrong. Gandhi made a patriot out of every Indian who joined the freedom movement.

As a result of Gandhi's soaring popularity, more and more Indians began to muster the courage to point out their yearning for freedom to the British. The fear of inferiority complex of Indians against the British on which the empire was built stood challenged by Gandhi's belief in the victory of good over evil, but the gulf between Hindus and Muslims and the communal factors in Indian politics were so strong that the movement ended up tearing India into two parts.

Sometimes, we get so carried away by the urge to prove our patriotism that we tend to ignore the purpose it serves. It is common among sports fans, for example, to identify themselves as patriots. They take pride in singing their national anthems and in waving their flags with all their might while the players represent their countries on the field. It helps create and strengthen the sense of national unity and pride and serves to boost the confidence of the players who represent them and their fellow countrymen. But for the actual players, it may be entirely different. They have a purpose to achieve, i.e., to give their best in the game they are in and to achieve the highest glory for their nation. They may be encouraged by the cheering of the supporters who gather to watch the games, but the desire to bring glory to their nations often enables them to surpass their own abilities and create new benchmarks.

In India's case too, there were the cheerers for freedom as well as the real players. Freedom fighters, revolutionaries and political leaders fell in the latter category, but the common people on the streets and in the villages were in the former. A sense of purpose is likely to give direction to any sentiment. Patriotism seems very fluid in this regard and while one may feel patriotic all the time, a sense of purpose gives him/her an adrenaline rush of sorts to do the patriotic thing. The mass movement that Gandhi helped build in India was brewing with energy but was still not quite clear in its sense of purpose as people continued to disagree among themselves over the idea of the nation that they were fighting to free.

Those at the forefront of the battle against the British were fighting in all possible ways, but for many, the purpose for their fight was vague. In other words, leaders wanted to do everything they could to end British rule but were not quite sure what that would lead to. It was fanciful to imagine that all suffering would end once the British were gone but it was far from reality. More importantly, the purpose of freedom was not unified among all people and leading political icons of that time.

Many prominent leaders as well as ordinary folks looked at Islam as something that had arrived in India as an invader, plundered the country's wealth, attempted to wipe out its cultural and religious ethos, and carried out numerable sins against the native population. They believed that Muslims had no claim over the country that even they were fighting to free. The Gandhian view, on the other hand, held that the Muslims in the 1900s were not responsible for the errors of the past and that they should be treated equally and at par with the rest of the Indians. It was also significant because unity in diversity could be the best possible answer to the British's divide and rule.

Patriotism in the Indian subcontinent too went the English way when the idea of independence was sought to be manipulated in favour of a Hindu-majoritarian State, and later when Mohammed Ali Jinnah's call for Pakistan gained momentum and ultimately led to the partition of India into two separate countries. Pakistan was born as a free land for the Muslims because of what the Pakistanis claimed as the prevailing fear of their rights being subjugated in a majoritarian State that India would emerge into after its independence.

Gandhi stood against this idea. He called for the unity of all Indians, irrespective of their caste, creed or religion. But not all were satisfied with the creation of a nation on secular values. Gandhi urged his fellow patriots to acknowledge the fact that Muslims who believed in the idea of a free India were as much Indians as Hindus or people belonging to other religions. The extremist leaders viewed Gandhian principles as the key challenge to the creation of Pakistan's replica in India.

This signified that there was an idea of India that was opposed to what independent India later came to represent. Gandhi was the calm breeze in this rough winter avalanche when the fight for dominance had turned into bigotry and hate had come to prevail over the subcontinent at large. The composure with which he led the country through this tumultuous phase earned him the title of 'Mahatma'. The fight was for freedom, but the Mahatma saw that the two communities were only shackling themselves, fearful of each other. He taught Indians to accept each other for who they were, to respect each other and to work collectively towards the shared objective. This objective was not mere attainment of freedom but also ensuring that the country marched into a civilized future instead of fighting among its own people. This was the purpose that patriotism sought to serve in its formative years in India.

When communal disharmony spiked in the wake of the call for Pakistan, Gandhi sat on numerous fasts to convince his people to shed violence and accept each other. He taught Indians that it was possible for Hindus and Muslims to live peacefully, that shedding the burden of the past was better than plunging into a hateful future and that there was no reason why they should nurture difference for one another in their hearts. And he made sense to people, which is perhaps why independent India emerged as a nation whose larger population held on to his views for decades to follow. Songs and hymns such as '*Raghupati Raghav Raja Ram*' and '*Saare Jahan Se Accha*' were sung regularly at prayer meetings that Gandhi attended to impart the values of harmony and brotherhood among people. To Gandhi, India was one people with all the differences they had among them and his message of peace, harmony and non-violence, which, he said, was also in sync with ancient Indian culture and ethos, found numerous takers in the land where the Ganges flows.

Another significant difference was on the principle of whether violence could be the means of achieving freedom. In his attempt to lead the country into a peaceful and harmonious future, Gandhi regarded the idea of violence as something that was alien to ancient India and, therefore, sought to portray non-violence as not only the driving force of India's freedom movement but also the natural flow of Indian cultural and historical practices. He seemed to suggest that violence was a myth to Indian culture while also stressing that Indians had long been living peacefully and that they should adhere to the same method of achieving freedom. Non-violence, or ahimsa, as the method of opposing British imperialism and harmonious coexistence among Indians of all religions and differences, was at the centre of the Gandhian ideology that helped India attain its freedom.

On the other hand, there was no dearth of revolutionaries, bravehearts and radical leaders too. We should also note that while all violent uprisings were systematically crushed by the British due to their disunity among Indians, the non-violent mass movement led by Gandhi succeeded because of its clever use of democratic and human rights issues. Apart from uniting people in India, Gandhi also ran what can today be described as a global PR exercise. He challenged the British by showing a mirror to them and pointing out quite clearly that they were violating the very ideals in India which they were fighting to secure in Germany and elsewhere. It was a battle fought on principles and Gandhi knew that two wrongs could not make a right.

Revered historian Upinder Singh, daughter of former Indian prime minister Dr Manmohan Singh, contends that the problem of political violence in India has hardly been noticed. She says that the great value attached to non-violence in Gandhian philosophy lulled us into thinking of a non-violent ancient India.

Singh told this writer in an interview:

This is a myth… Ancient Indian history is full of episodes of bloody wars, succession struggles, patricide, fratricide, conflicts between states and forest people, and the killing of animals. There was also social conflict. These things are well known, but we have somehow not joined the dots. Ancient India boasts the icons of ahimsa like Mahavira, the Buddha and Ashoka. But what people need to realize is that their strong pleas for non-violence indicate that these men were very troubled by violence all around them. So, the idea of a non-violent ancient India is indeed a myth. This pleasant myth can perhaps offer some comfort in our desire for peace and harmony in our present violent, intolerant, conflict-ridden world. It can be used as a basis to argue for a return to a golden age of non-violence. But such a golden age never existed. Such myths are not history and it is necessary to demolish them.[8]

The question in front of India was more daunting than simply crippling the British empire. It was not only about attaining freedom but also about building the nation after freedom, which is perhaps why progressive Indian leaders, with Gandhi at the forefront, led their countrymen into believing that their violent past should not prevent them from forging more harmonious and peaceful ways for our present and the future. Independence

---

[8]Saket Suman, '"The idea of a non-violent ancient India is a myth": Historian Upinder Singh,' *The News Minute*, 17 October 2017, https://www.thenewsminute.com/article/idea-non-violent-ancient-india-myth-historian-upinder-singh-70134, accessed 8 May 2021.

was not going to be the end of the road, as the nation that patriots were fighting to free would have to be built from scratch.

A student of St. Mary's High School in Pune was on a sublime quest in the 1940s as it was the most exciting time in her life so far. Every day after school, she would cross the street with a bunch of friends and go to Dr Mehta's Nature Cure Clinic, where Gandhi held his prayer meetings. The clinic was not very far from her home and so she went quite often to listen to Gandhi. It was almost customary for the crusader of India's non-violent freedom movement to address such gatherings and spread his messages. Hymns of communal harmony would be sung at these gatherings and Gandhi would call upon his fellow citizens to accept each other and work collectively.

Nonetheless, the young girl's father was an army doctor and he was worried that his daughter attending the meetings of the man who was spearheading the Indian independence movement could have repercussions on his job. But the little girl cared the least as the entire mood at that time was tremendously exciting.

'We did not know what it was all about because one was too young to really understand it fully. But one knew that something very substantial was happening and one was aware that a major change was about to come,' she recalls.

One day, she managed to get an autograph of the Mahatma and just after Bapu had signed it, he said something, *'Yeh resham ke kapde pehne hue hain?* (Are you wearing silk?)' 'Yes,' she replied. Gandhi looked at her closely and then said: 'Never wear silk or anything made in the mills, you must always wear khadi. So, go back now and tell your parents to get you khadi clothes and wear only clothes that are made of khadi.'

She would go on to become one of the most reputed, but

equally controversial, historians of India—Romila Thapar.[9] She was still a child, but Gandhi's words had touched her. When she returned home that night, she told her parents that she must completely overhaul her wardrobe from then on. Her mother was annoyed. 'Here she goes with another fangirl idea,' she said. But her father understood. 'Look, forget it. Get her two salwar kurtas made of khadi, she will wear them for two months and then she will get over it,' he told her mother to settle the issue.

'And that's exactly what happened,' Thapar recalls.

This awe-inspiring meeting at such an early age with the man who would later become the Father of the Nation is etched permanently in Thapar's mind. In 1947, she was in the last year of her schooling. There was excitement everywhere, not because it was the final year of school but because the colonial rule in India was soon to end and a new dawn waited ahead.

'My last year of school was 1947. It was an experience of tremendous excitement because one was in one's teens and the whole conversation around was the national movement and the coming of Independence and how things would change and one was sort of waiting for something dramatic to happen, which would lead to independence taking place,' she recalls.

With nationalism at its peak and independence of India fast approaching, most conversations that young Romila had during those days were centred around the national movement and

---

[9]Saket Suman, 'I write what I think is right, give my evidence take it or leave it: Historian Romila Thapar,' *The Quint*, 5 March 2018, https://www.thequint.com/news/hot-news/i-write-what-i-think-is-right-give-my-evidence-take-it-or-leave-it-historian-romila-thapar, accessed 8 May 2021.

national leaders, and the events that were taking place at that time. 'There were many more complaints about the British rule than there had been before because people were a little quiet before that. But as soon as the idea of independence approached and it soon became a reality, then people started speaking much more,' she says. It was the excitement of building a new society.

'The conversations at the dinner table at home were about the new country and what would be the expected changes in various areas after Independence and what would happen after the change.'

About three weeks before 15 August 1947, the day India became independent, Thapar was called by Sister Superior of her school.

'You are one of the Indian prefects and we would want you to be present on the 15th,' Sister Superior told her. 'What we would like you to do is bring down the Union Jack and put up the Indian flag, plant a little tree to mark the occasion and then make a speech.'

Everything else seemed exciting for young Romila but not making a speech.

She had participated in school debates and other similar functions, but this was going to be different. She had to make a speech and the entire school, along with guardians and visitors were going to be present. At first, she resented it.

'Make a speech? What am I going to say?' she asked.

But Sister Superior insisted that she had to do it—a speech of about 15 minutes.

'For the next three weeks, I went around thinking what I was going to say! It was a frightening thought, the entire school, all parents, friends and everybody was going to be there. It was going to be a big occasion. I remember getting more and more desperate about what I was going to say till I went to have a chat with my favourite teacher, who happened to teach literature and history,' adds Thapar.

She was advised to 'just sit down and think about the conversations that you have with your friends about the coming of Independence. What do you expect from Independence? And just talk about that'.

And then finally, 15 August 1947 arrived. A new nation was born and Thapar delivered her first speech. She recalls that she spoke about two primary things. One was about the kind of society that 'we were going to have after Independence' because the British were not going to be there and therefore the entire living pattern was going to change. The second thing that she spoke about was 'how are we then going to adapt' to all the changes that were happening around at that point of time.

This was how a young Indian looked at the coming of Independence. It was a great moment, a tryst with destiny, as Pandit Jawaharlal Nehru, independent India's first prime minister, described in his famous speech at the stroke of midnight. But the culmination of the prevalent communal hatred resulted in the partition of India and tore a timeless civilization into two parts: India and Pakistan.

Both nations were built on their own ideals. In India, there was a place for everybody and the bloodshed that followed Partition, irrespective of which side it was from, was condemned and not celebrated. Independent India was poor, starving and robbed of all its wealth. It had to feed an increasing population while also laying down the foundation of modern educational and scientific infrastructure. It had to ensure its security against not-very-kind neighbours. And to do all of this, it had very little resources at its disposal while its population was still nurturing discrimination among themselves.

There was an idea opposed to that of Gandhi and the independent Indian establishment under Nehru. This idea, though staunchly opposed to Pakistan, was also built on a similar religious line, and found resonance among the Hindu fundamentalists. They resented that they did not get a Hindu Rashtra while the Muslims got their own separate country. And there were harsh memories of the past too. The glorious Mughal dynasty thrived because of its atrocities on the native population, they believed, and therefore demanded the ouster of Muslims from India. But Gandhi was an obstacle. He stood for everything that his opponents opposed. Gandhi stood for peace, he stood for harmony, he stood for equality and he believed in the power of the people. Patriotism in India was so emerging in those battered days that acceptance had to become a norm more than a necessity. The fabric of India could only remain united if internal biases and discriminations could be shed.

But then, 30 January 1948 was just another day. Romila Thapar was young and she was still living in Pune. All of a sudden, she sensed strange chaos in the air, steeped in some kind of confusion. She could not comprehend what was happening around her as all she could hear was everybody asking one another: 'Do you know what happened? Did you hear about what happened?'

People put on their radios and found out that Gandhi had been assassinated. Thapar says her immediate reaction was, 'My God! Who was it?'

It was a shocking moment for her and even seven decades after the heinous act was committed, she remembers quite vividly the emotions she felt upon hearing the news.

'One did feel very sad. The little contact that you have with someone creates a tiny bond, a very tiny bond. I just kept sitting there and thinking that he was such a gentle person; why would anybody think of assassinating him? Go up and argue with him, abuse him if you want but don't assassinate him. I simply could not come to terms with that,' she contends.

There were already apprehensions about who might have killed him. The memory of Partition was still fairly fresh and people were still very frightened at the thought of any act of violence because the communal riots that had surfaced in its worst forms would come back again. 'And then they announced that the assassin was actually a Hindu' and that put an entirely different perspective to it.

The world grieved when the Mahatma died. *The Statesman* noted:

> Mahatma Gandhi was not merely a great nationalist but perhaps a greater internationalist, proving by action that the two are not incompatible. He was unique in evolving, and in rendering world-famous, a weapon novel in modern times with which to fight, the weapon of non-violence.
>
> The world may soon find it has no alternative, because of the horrifying new means of slaughter now developed. Whether the nations come to their senses in time, or are engulfed in atomic war, Mahatma Gandhi will stand pre-eminent in this century as the man who not only saw, before most others, the calamitous objectives to which

violence of its nature tends, but who made practical efforts on an unprecedentedly large scale to provide an alternative.[10]

A nation that was born out of numerous sacrifices and struggles had let its tallest icon down. The principles and values that the Mahatma sought to instill in the hearts and minds of his fellow citizens came across as a threat to the proclamation of a different understanding and vision of India. This vision wanted the creation of a Hindu Rashtra, or a Hindu Nation, for its majority population. Everything that could go wrong had gone wrong within months of India's independence as Indians still struggled to arrive at a consensus and give a definitive meaning and objective to patriotism.

But Gandhi did not come to be hailed as the Father of the Nation for nothing. The values he stood for struck a chord with most Indians, and they were saddened at his assassination. Gandhi came to be regarded in high esteem in India and abroad. He became the face of every currency note in the country and so magnanimous would be his influence over Indian politics that generations of politicians in the following decades would cling on to his clothing and ideals, at least in their public persona, whereas his assassin, Nathuram Godse, emerged as the first villain in independent India. Godse would become a symbol of who not to be, whereas even Gandhi's critics would find solace in his principles and vision of India.

Gandhi's death was a great blow to India, but it did not

---

[10]'Tributes to Gandhiji,' Gandhi Heritage Portal, *The Statesman*, Calcutta, https://www.gandhiheritageportal.org/tribute-detail/NjQ=/NjY=, accessed 10 May 2021.

mark the end of the road for our great nation. It was instead the beginning of a new chapter that would be built on his teachings, which would regard his ideals as national ethos and abide by them while also honouring him as the Father of the Nation. He paid the ultimate sacrifice for peace and the well-being of his fellow citizens and yet never harnessed an iota of hate for his opponents. Gandhi was all for debates and discussions; however, knives and revolvers had more sway over those who were opposed to him. Gandhi believed in equality of all whereas, because their ambition of superiority on religious lines had been forsaken forever under Gandhian leadership of the Indian freedom movement, the fundamentalists loathed him.

In his tribute to Gandhi, Nehru's words are worth recalling:

Great men and eminent men have monuments in bronze and marble set up for them, but this man of divine fire managed in his lifetime to become enmeshed in millions and millions of hearts so that all of us became somewhat of the stuff that he was made of, though to an infinitely lesser degree. He spread out over India not in palaces only, or in select places, or in assemblies, but in every hamlet and hut of the lowly and those who suffer. He lives in the hearts of millions and he will live for immemorial ages. He has gone, and all over India there is a feeling of having been left desolate and forlorn...In ages to come, centuries and maybe millenniums after us, people will think of this generation when this man of God trod the earth and will think of us who, however small, could also follow his path and probably tread on that holy ground where his feet had been. Let us be worthy of him. Let us always be so.[11]

And this marked the path India would chart for itself in the years and decades to come.

---

[11]'Tributes to Gandhiji,' Gandhi Heritage Portal, https://www. gandhiheritageportal.org/tributes-to-gandhiji/by-pandit-jawaharlal-nehru, accessed 10 May 2021.

3

We the People

Susannah and Shashi grew up in independent India of the 1960s, barely a decade after Independence. Shashi was born in London to a middle-class family, which returned to India soon after his birth, while Susannah was born in Shillong, and the surrounding hills were the first sights young Susie saw, quite unaware of their magnificence. It was nothing like the London of today, 'but whatever it may have been', Shashi says, he has 'very little memory of those days', as his family moved back to India when he was barely 'two, two-and-a-half or three years old'. He was confined to bed due to asthma; she was restless, lonely and broken from early on. They were both living their lives in the course of the nation.

Ours was a young nation, and one of the challenges was to open its people to the larger world and the reality of the times they were living in. Universities and colleges, refineries, dams and industries were being set up across the country after centuries of plunder at the hands of the empire. People were eager to contribute their bit towards the cause of nation-building. There were doctors, police, military, teachers, nurses and the common citizens. Patriotism symbolized different things to them, but the sense of being Indian was also very much alive.

The new generation had made minimal contributions towards Independence, many weren't even born at that time. They were born as Indians and that became their identity. This sacred bond of the people with the patria was documented in the Constitution of India, which they hoped to live up to. Quite evidently, the battles of the past were meant to end with Independence as India became a free land for everybody, regardless of their religion, caste, creed or gender. The Hindu-Muslim gulf and the post-Partition communal disharmony were the daunting challenges the nation would strive to overcome in the following years.

At the same time, there were thousands of poor and deprived, those who had been forsaken by society—suppressed, neglected or forced to live on the periphery. Independent India meant that they were as much a part of the country as the privileged elite, the upper castes or the freedom fighters too, for that matter. In fact, it became almost binding for the State to build an inclusive society. Unlike many European countries, patriotism in India did not necessarily signify any singular view. India was not formed on either religious or linguistic lines. Pakistan, though formed on communal grounds, fell prey to the disregard it showed to linguistic difference between its eastern and western parts.

In every democratic country, the laws governing the land apply to all citizens, regardless of their differences or diversities.

In India's case, most of the laws were formulated in Britain during the nineteenth century. With the passage of time, representation was granted to Indian leaders, but the actual powers still rested in the hands of the British. The transfer of power took place in 1947, but India's own laws came into effect a little later. The law of the land became the embodiment of the legal authority the people empowered to govern them.

The Constitution of India had involved a rigorous process that was aimed at ensuring that the power always remained in the hands of the people. It was also important to have a constitution specifically meant for its people, which is why, despite imbibing quite significantly from several other constitutions around the world, the Indian Constitution stood out for its specific consideration of minorities, the deprived, as well as the indigenous tribes.

It was, in fact, made amply clear during the very first meeting of the Constituent Assembly that India's constitution had to be so drafted that it became naturally acceptable to its people. Nehru famously told the august gathering that India was not just going to copy ideals, procedures and provisions of the constitution from elsewhere.[12]

'Whatever system of government we may establish here must fit in with the temper of our people and be acceptable to them. We stand for democracy,' Nehru had said in a speech while outlining the vision of the Indian Constitution on 13 December 1946.

---

[12]Sudarshan Agarwal, *Jawaharlal Nehru and Rajya Sabha*, Prentice-Hall of India Private Limited, 1989, https://rajyasabha.nic.in/rsnew/publication_electronic/Jawaharlal.pdf, accessed 10 May 2021.

The purpose of that meeting was to draw the objectives of the Constitution of India, which Nehru had drafted and moved in the Constituent Assembly on that occasion. Based on these objectives emerged the Preamble to the Constitution of India, which describes the aspirations of the Indian people. It is a very crisp introductory statement, which became a guide to patriotism in India as it set forth the relationship between the State and its people with astounding clarity. It also represented the principles and the ethos of the Constitution as well as the source from which the document derived its authority and meaning.

The reason why young Indians later did not feel the Constitution was forcefully thrust upon them and came to accept it quite naturally was because the drafting committee and the Constituent Assembly went into every little detail and discussed all major issues of contention before they were accepted as a part of the Constitution.

Noted author and activist Seth Govind Das, for example, highlighted the cultural background to the protection of cows, and why it is regarded as mata (mother) in India.

> Ours is an agricultural country. It should have all that is necessary for agriculture. From this point of view, the protection of cows is very essential for us. The problem of cow protection is a matter which has been associated with our civilisation from the time of Lord Krishna. To us, it is not only a religious or economic but also a cultural problem. Just as we have declared the practice of untouchability an offence, we can also declare that cow-slaughter in this country would be an offence. We should

include some provision in our Constitution for this. We learn from our history that only such regimes, whether during Hindu period or Muslim period, as had prohibited cow-slaughter had been popular and successful in our country. History is a witness to the fact that cow-slaughter was abolished here during the rule of many Muslim Kings. It may be said that it would entail a heavy financial burden. I submit, however, that even if we impose a tax on the people and ask them to pay it in order to protect the cows, I am of the opinion that they would pay it quite willingly. The bogey of financial difficulties used to be raised before us by the British Government. But I would like that in the matter of cow-protection this bogey should not be raised before us by the British government.[13]

Similarly, Damodar Swarup Seth, the staunch socialist and a Constituent Assembly member, had highlighted the key role played by Gandhi in making the Indian freedom struggle a mass movement. He noted that the Constitution should consider Gandhian philosophies and avoid centralization of power. A staunch socialist, he went to the extent of stating that the Assembly should be dissolved as it didn't represent all sections of the Indian society.

Seth, an outspoken defender of the rights of people from the economically and socially lower strata of the society, warned us about the ill effects of centralization of power. He had said:

---

[13]Constituent Assembly of India debates (proceedings), Volume VII, 5 November 1948, http://164.100.47.194/Loksabha/Debates/cadebatefiles/C05111948.html, accessed 20 May 2021.

Centralization is a good thing and is useful at times but we forget that all through his life, Mahatma Gandhi emphasised the fact that too much centralization of power makes that power totalitarian and takes it towards fascist ideals. The only method of safeguarding against totalitarianism and fascism is that power should be decentralized to the greatest extent. We would have thus brought about such a centralization of power through welding of heart as could not be matched anywhere in the world. But the natural consequence of centralising power by law will be that our country which has all along opposed Fascism—even today we claim to strongly oppose it—will gradually move towards Fascism.[14]

While it was naturally expected of the citizens of the independent nation to behave as patriots, the fear of sedition also lurked among the members of the Constituent Assembly, which is perhaps why the matter was vigorously debated during the formation of the Indian Consitution. Prominent members such as K.M Munshi, popularly known by his pen name Ghanshyam Vyas, expressed that criticism of the government should not be seen as sedition. But the most significant exchange on the matter took place between the Sikh leader Bhopinder Singh Mann and the Speaker of the Constituent Assembly, Seth Govind Das.

Mann warned the august gathering thus:

---

[14]Constituent Assembly of India debates (proceedings), Volume VII, 5 November 1948, https://www.constitutionofindia.net/constitution_assembly_debates/volume/7/1948-11-05, accessed 20 May 2021.

For the public in general, and for the minorities in particular, I attach great importance to association and to free speech. It is through them that we can make our voice felt by the Government, and can stop the injustice that might be done to us. For attaining these rights, the country had to make so many struggles, and after a grim battle succeeded in getting these rights recognised. But now, when the time for their enforcement has come, the Government feels hesitant; what was deemed as undesirable then is now being paraded as desirable. What is being given by one hand is being taken away by the other.[15]

Das, who was a noted Satyagrahi and had been jailed several times, recalled that his grandfather held the title of 'Raja' while his uncle and father held the title of 'Diwan Bahadur'. He said:

I am very glad that titles will no more be granted in this country. In spite of belonging to such a family, I was prosecuted under Section 124A and that also for an interesting thing. My great grandfather had been awarded a gold waistband inlaid with diamonds. The British Government awarded it to him for helping it in 1857 and the words, 'In recognition of his services during the Mutiny in 1857' were engraved on it. In the course of my speech during the Satyagraha movement of 1930, I said that my great-grandfather got this waistband for helping

---

[15]Constituent Assembly debates, Official report, Volume VII, 2 December 1948, https://eparlib.nic.in/bitstream/123456789/762991/1/cad_02-12-1948. pdf, accessed 20 May 2021.

the alien government and that he had committed a sin by doing so and that I wanted to have engraved on it that the sin committed by my great-grandfather in helping to keep such a government in existence had been expiated by the great-grandson by seeking to uproot it. For this, I was prosecuted under Section 124A and sentenced to two years' rigorous imprisonment.[16]

The members recognized that the only reason why sedition was weaved into the Indian Penal Code (IPC) in 1870 was to jail the critics of the British Raj. Therefore, at the very outset, it became amply clear that the matter of sedition or treachery towards the cause of the motherland wasn't something that was ignored by the founders of the Republic of India. It was instead hotly debated, argued and deliberated upon. The members of the Constituent Assembly, after much thought and reflection, believed that the struggle for freedom was based on the idea of liberty and thus the entire exercise would turn futile if citizens of independent India were forbidden from criticizing their own elected government for the fear of sedition. Criticizing the government of the day was not an anti-national act to their mind and to the spirit of the Indian Constitution.

As originally enacted, the Preamble describes India as a 'sovereign democratic republic'. The Preamble to the Constitution of India describes in great detail the relationship the State shares with its people. That is the premise from which Indian patriotism derives its meaning. People were not only

---

[16]Constituent Assembly Debates on 2 December 1948. Part I, https://indiankanoon.org/docfragment/1389880/?big=0&formInput=sedition%20%20doctypes:%20debates, accessed 18 May 2021.

reading the words but were actually trying to live that life. Many adjustments were being made, people were trying to adapt to freedom, they were learning to live with each other and withstand the forces that wished otherwise.

It was because of such foresight and vision of the founding fathers of our nation that the coming generation was blessed to breathe free air, dwell upon a free land and emerge as free thinkers in a free country. The India that Shashi gained consciousness in was therefore a very liberal and cosmopolitan environment. His father had dropped his caste surname during the nationalist movement; his parents brought him up never knowing his caste until some kid asked him at school. He had Muslim friends, Christian friends, Parsi friends and Hindu friends and he never knew the difference, nor was he ever made to feel it by his parents, he says. National integration, as he saw it, was not just a slogan; there was a very clear consciousness that if they had to be something better as a nation, then they needed to aim at their better natures and they had to overcome the bitter divisions of Partition.

'That was the India I grew up in as a child and, therefore, those are the values that I stuck with,' he elaborates.

It was a great feat that became a possibility because India's constitution was the outcome of the sacred resolution of the Indian people to constitute their country into a 'sovereign democratic republic'. It was realized to secure several well-defined objectives, which were laid down in the Preamble's text. These were legacies to future generations of Indians, they would be required to live up to these ideals and values and thrive and prosper as they made a life for themselves.

The Constitution of India came into effect on 26 January

1950, which is now celebrated as Republic Day by Indians across the world.

During the course of the making of India's constitution, members debated each of its aspects, which were then reported and critiqued in newspapers. The views of the general public as also those of ethnic minorities and religious groups were invited, discussed and deliberated upon. These led to debates on justice, which in turn, resulted in a representation of voices from the marginalized sections of society. It was not an ordinary document. In fact, the pages of the original constitution were designed and decorated by the revered painter Beohar Rammanohar Sinha and Acharya Nandalal Bose. The calligraphy was done by Prem Behari Narain Raizada.

It is easy to think of patriotism as something very outward, aggressive and outspoken but not quite so to really apply its meaning in the life of people. While Shashi's India was a liberal and cosmopolitan environment, Susannah's world was very different. He had a privileged childhood, she was deprived of all that he often took for granted. This contrast began way too early in their separate lives, as it happens in almost every town, city, village or hamlet across India. It may break your hearts at the absolute unfairness of our brutal world but deep down under its currents, it secretly hides the unseen forces that shape our notions towards loyalty and rebellion. He had so much to be proud of and to boast about, she had very little to show off and thump her chest.

Although we do not see it that way when we think of patriotism, it is almost always the case with humans that our world begins with our mother. It is the thoughts and reflections in the innermost chambers of her heart that shapes and moulds our earliest perspectives. The bond we share with her is our utmost sense of belonging when we are in that most vulnerable, albeit innocent, stage of childhood. Susannah's mother, she recalls, is not just any woman. She is the most crazy, violent and wonderful woman she knows. There are many facets of her and she unleashed them completely upon young Susie. But then, the gentle child could also sense the vulnerability that they were faced with in the world where they had no protection at all and anything could happen to them at any time. They were like two nuclear powers in the same room and Susannah's upbringing under her mother's shadows instilled a child-like wonder in her heart, making her delight in the lesser things of creation.

Shashi's mother, on the other hand, was a voracious reader and would read out from Enid Blyton's *Noddy* books to him, and Shashi, she often jokes, would snatch the book from her and begin reading for himself. His mother had the highest expectations of him. Nothing that Shashi did during his early days seemed 'good enough' for his mother. She seldom congratulated him on winning prizes and distinctions too. 'They were expected,' he says as she would herself drive her son to debate and quiz competitions and routinely take him to All India Radio stations to participate in children's programmes. He became a precocious debater and extempore speaker at school and college, as well as a regular on the amateur theatrical stage, winning his Bombay school's Best Actor Award three years in a row. These experiences prepared him for public life from a very young age.

There was, however, a sense of anxiety in Susannah's immediate surroundings because even though they were not at the bottom of the caste ladder, there was a sort of understanding that nobody was going to marry her. There was a constant pressure on her, she was repeatedly reminded of her caste and social stature. That she was not a pure Syrian Christian breed. That she had no money to pay the dowry. And yet, the promise of Independence was being lived because she could see 'that once people gained education, they were actually able to transform their lives'. One could break through the societal barriers and the very realization of this fact by a young girl underlines the greatness of our constitutional spirit, which constantly seeks to remind us of equality even though our world had and has been turning increasingly unequal.

While the spread of the constitutional ethos and its full implication at the grass-roots level remained a distant dream, it could also not change the fact that 'We the People' had made it the law of the land. In other words, if patriotism was rebellious in its avatar during the quest for freedom, the coming of Independence along with the adoption of the Constitution ensured that people of India became loyal towards the law of the land.

> *WE, THE PEOPLE OF INDIA, having solemnly resolved to constitute India into a [SOVEREIGN SOCIALIST SECULAR DEMOCRATIC REPUBLIC] and to secure to all its citizens: JUSTICE, social, economic and political; LIBERTY of thought, expression, belief, faith and worship; EQUALITY of status and of opportunity; and to promote among them all FRATERNITY assuring the dignity of the individual and the [unity and integrity of the Nation]; IN OUR CONSTITUENT ASSEMBLY this twenty-sixth day*

of November, 1949, do HEREBY ADOPT, ENACT AND GIVE TO OURSELVES THIS CONSTITUTION.[17]

For a patriot in India, therefore, whatever sacrifices or actions patriotism demanded naturally came to be seen in line with the constitutional norms. Patriotism was essential to protect the Constitution and to safeguard four fundamental elements that we generally overlook. These elements are discussed as follows.

Justice, which denotes the rule of law and the absence of arbitrariness as well as a system of equal rights and opportunities, had found due mention in the Constitution, which made it almost binding upon the State to seek social, economic and political justice in order to ensure equality to its citizens. It demanded the absence of socially privileged classes in society and the prohibition of discrimination against any citizen on the grounds of caste, creed, colour, religion, gender or place of birth. Independent India had decided to eliminate such exploitations from its society. It also realized that no discrimination between man and woman on the basis of income, wealth and economic status would be made in its territory. And most importantly, the Preamble also granted political justice, which denotes its will to grant equal, free and fair opportunities to the people for participation in the political process. In this regard, all Indians should have equal political rights without discrimination.

Then there is the idea of Liberty, which implies that there should be no unreasonable restrictions on Indian citizens with

---

[17]The 42nd Amendment in 1976 amended the Preamble and changed the description of India from 'sovereign democratic republic' to a 'sovereign, socialist secular democratic republic', and also changed the words 'unity of the nation' to 'unity and integrity of the nation'.

regard to what they think, their manner of expression and the way they wish to follow up their thoughts into action, while adhering to the constitutional limitations.

The idea of Equality envisaged that no section of the Indian society would enjoy special privileges and that all individuals are provided with adequate opportunities without any form of discrimination. In other words, every Indian is equal before the law. Equality specifically denoted the end of privileges or discrimination against any section of the society. The Preamble provided for equality of status and opportunity to all the people of the country.

And we should not forget Fraternity, which refers to a feeling of brotherhood and a sense of belongingness towards India among its people. It envelops psychological as well as territorial dimensions and is essential for the national integration of the country because a feeling of goodwill and shared identity may keep it together. Fraternity explicitly forbids or seeks to forbid divisive factors such as regionalism, communalism and casteism.

The framers of India's constitution had ensured that it respected the freedom of diverse views too. It was a daunting ambition, as daunting as the struggle for freedom, but India strived to be worthy of the Mahatma. It was also not extraordinary that the Constitution of India demolished the ambitions of a Hindu-majoritarian State in India, the equivalent for Hindus what Pakistan was for Muslims. It happened after Gandhi's death, but the Constitution of India was the final nail in the coffin for such ambitions.

Dr B.R. Ambedkar, who had come to be regarded as the 'Father of the Constitution of India' remarked about the Preamble of the Indian Constitution thus:

It was, indeed, a way of life, which recognizes liberty, equality and fraternity as the principles of life and which cannot be divorced from each other: Liberty cannot be divorced from equality; equality cannot be divorced from liberty. Nor can liberty and equality be divorced from fraternity. Without equality, liberty would produce the supremacy of the few over the many. Equality without liberty would kill individual initiative. Without fraternity, liberty and equality could not become a natural course of things.[18]

The 389 members of the Constituent Assembly, which was reduced to 299 after the Partition, worked tirelessly for about three years under Ambedkar's leadership to prepare the document that became the supreme law of the land. Ambedkar himself studied in great detail the constitutions of about 60 countries, and though the Indian Constitution borrowed quite significantly from them, it was structured in a manner that it reflected the natural aspirations of the Indian people.

Tiruvellore Thattai Krishnamachari, an entrepreneur and prominent leader, who was also a member of the Drafting Committee, had appropriately highlighted the unparalleled role played by Ambedkar in giving the Indian Constitution its full shape.

Mr President, Sir, I am one of those in the House who have listened to Dr Ambedkar very carefully. I am aware of

---

[18]'The Grammar of Anarchy,' *Outlook*, 20 January 2014, https://www.outlookindia.com/website/story/the-grammar-of-anarchy/289235, accessed 16 June 2021.

the amount of work and enthusiasm that he has brought to bear on the work of drafting this Constitution. At the same time, I do realise that that amount of attention [sic] that was necessary for the purpose of drafting a constitution so important to us at this moment has not been given to it by the Drafting Committee. The House is perhaps aware that of the seven members nominated by you, one had resigned from the House and was replaced. One died and was not replaced. One was away in America and his place was not filled up and another person was engaged in State affairs, and there was a void to that extent. One or two people were far away from Delhi and perhaps reasons of health did not permit them to attend. So it happened ultimately that the burden of drafting this constitution fell on Dr Ambedkar and I have no doubt that we are grateful to him for having achieved this task in a manner which is undoubtedly commendable.[19]

Krishnamachari later served as Finance Minister from 1956–58 and from 1964–66, and he also had the ignominy of being the first minister in free India to have resigned due to his involvement in a scam.

Think of it from the perspective of the people of independent India, somebody who may not have been a well-known freedom fighter but a common citizen on the street who was equally proud of its freedom struggle. He/she could be anybody—a Hindu, a Muslim, a Sikh, a Christian, a Harijan, differently

[19]Constituent Assembly of India debates (proceedings), Volume VII, 5 November 1948, https://www.constitutionofindia.net/constitution_assembly_debates/volume/7/1948-11-05, accessed 31 May 2021.

abled, a tribal, an Anglo-Indian and so on and so forth. He/she could be from anywhere—Assam, Kerala, Bengal, Maharashtra, Bihar and the rest. Besides, there were linguistic and cultural diversities too. The entirety of India was not made up by Hindus alone and not all Hindus believed in the creation of a Hindi-Hindu-Hindustan sort of nation. This list started with none less than the Mahatma himself. In fact, it is also worth noting that most members of the Constituent Assembly were also elected representatives of the people and they shunned the idea of a Hindu Rashtra because it had profound drawbacks and was inappropriate for a land of such diversities, as also because of the prevailing social discriminations in society. They instead chose to build a liberal and pluralistic society.

The Indian Constitution was an incredible document that defined the rights of the people as well as their relationship with the state because the members of the Constituent Assembly truly reflected the aspirations of the people. For Indians then, it was in the quest to transform constitutional guarantees into ground realities that patriotism must have manifested itself.

The Constitution did not regard India as a Hindu Rashtra, it became the edifice of a secular and democratic republic. The imposition of the majority view over the minorities, which were so many in number and in so many different forms, would result in another form of colonization, which is why the framers of the Indian Constitution had stressed upon the significance of justice, liberty, equality and fraternity in the Preamble.

Thus, in the Bombay of Shashi's boyhood, India was becoming a culture of cultures, a language of languages as its people seemed united by the beauty of their shared diversity. It had churches, temples, mosques, gurudwaras, stupas and more, but it chose to take pride in all of them. Its people spoke several languages and India recognized their right to do so and preserve what they thought was their mother tongue. It was similar with cultures and cuisines too, which is why Hyderabadi biryani or dosas from the South would become a sensation all over the country one day just as momos from the cold Himalayan regions or chole bhature from the North would travel to most cities across the length and breadth of the republic. This became a possibility because India became a democracy and democracies place power in the hands of the people by making them equal stakeholders in the union. In fact, patriotism is an essential element that has shaped our understanding of a democracy, though we do not quite look at it that way. Anarchy and monarchy, the two alternatives, were not only impractical in India but would also lead to a second term of colonization of sorts. Citizens surrender their patriotism in the form of loyalty to the crown in most monarchies, whereas an army of patriots, who are expected to act without reason, question or thought, enable larger-than-life demagogues to crush and suppress their citizens in anarchic regimes. Democracy is entirely different in the sense that power is vested in the people to elect their own government. If the freedom struggle was a yearning for independence, patriotism thereafter symbolized the struggle to retain the solemn bond people formed with the patria.

Indians were expected to regard the Constitution as the supreme law of the land, as also, look up to it as the manifestation of their patriotism while the nation, free from the clutches of imperialism, ushered in a new era in the emerging world order. In the meanwhile, patriotism remained unchallenged and enabled countries such as the United States and England to march on the path of what they defined as development. Those in power needed the military to fight their wars and taxes paid by people to fill their coffers. Patriotism helped keep this cycle running without a question. On the other hand, it also contributed to a great extent in the realization of the modern nation system, and in giving direction and objective to people. While all of this was happening, the yardstick of measuring the Constitution, which was drafted for India as a whole, and the manner in which it applied to people in reality continued to depend on several factors, including religion, caste, creed and other societal and economic barriers.

While the flags fly high and the national anthems are sung aloud, the misery of the common folk continues unabated in the abyss. In 1962, Susannah's parents separated and an uncertainty loomed large over their life. Her mother, Mary, was married to an assistant manager in a tea garden. But she was never in love with him and had married him, perhaps, to escape her fate in her own community. Although most think of divorce as a very terrible thing, for Susie, it was better to have a woman asserting her independence and growing into something wonderful like she later did rather than to live a life of suffering and to transmit that suffering on to her children. It wasn't easy, but she doesn't think it was a tragedy either. The broken family of three left the hilly terrains of Assam[20] and arrived in Kerala just around the time that our nation came to a grinding halt. The Chinese had attacked us and our freedom was once again at stake.

---

[20]Meghalaya was formed by carving out two districts from the state of Assam: the United Khasi Hills and Jaintia Hills, and the Garo Hills on 21 January 1972.

4

War and Peace

Even though people generally do not get to decide whether they want to be part of a war, the act of marching on in the face of adversity is dubbed as patriotism. War brings unimaginable horrors to the lives of people, who are impacted drastically without their slightest anticipation or control. Being a patriot does not mean beating our chests in victory or concealing stories of our defeat. It does not seek blind pride in martyrdom.

But then, for soldiers, armies and generals on the borders, patriotism is the way of life. They live to secure the promise of independence and guard the borders so that business can go about as usual. They enable countries to function effectively and are at the centre of things during times of war.

The world's two most populous countries—India and China—fought against each other in 1962. The mountainous border regions became the battlefield as China invaded India, bringing the entire nation to a state of complete disarray.

Nobody was really expecting it. '*Hindi Chini Bhai Bhai*' was the fancy quote being used by Indian diplomats during those days. Chinese and Indians were brothers, they said, but the error in judgement turned out to be quite fatal during the war. The Indian Army lacked a well-crafted military strategy against the Chinese troops and their advanced weapon systems.[21] The soldiers ran out of artillery, ammunition and food supplies.

The lofty mountain ranges of the Himalayas have served as the frontiers between India and its northern neighbours for centuries. However, the equations on the ground had changed significantly because India inherited boundary demarcations from the British, and China, being occupied by the communist forces in the late 1940s, sought to aggressively strengthen its strategic positioning.

After the Chinese annexed Tibet, it proclaimed that the entire Himalayan region was part of its sovereign territory. It refused to acknowledge the McMohan Line separating India from China in the east. It also laid claims on parts of Jammu and Kashmir. But, the two countries signed what became the Panchsheel or Five Principles of Agreement.[22] The Panchsheel was enunciated in the preamble to the Agreement (with exchange of notes) on Trade and Intercourse between Tibet

[21]Vikram Doctor, ET Bureau, '1962 India-China war: Why India needed that jolt,' *The Economic Times*, 7 October 2012, https://economictimes.indiatimes.com/news/politics-and-nation/1962-india-china-war-why-india-needed-that-jolt/articleshow/16703076.cms?from=mdr, accessed 10 May 2021.

[22]Prabhash K. Dutta, 'This day in 1962: China-India war started with synchronised attack on Ladakh, Arunachal,' *India Today*, 20 October 2017, https://www.indiatoday.in/india/story/india-china-war-1962-20-october-aksai-chin-nefa-arunchal-pradesh-1067703-2017-10-20, accessed 10 May 2021.

Region of China and India.

'All our old maps dealing with the frontier should be carefully examined, and where necessary, withdrawn. New maps should be printed showing our northern and northeastern frontier without any reference to any "line". These new maps should also not state there is any undemarcated territory,' Nehru had stated in a note to the Secretary-General and Foreign Secretary, Ministry of External Affairs, in 1954.[23]

'Both as flowing from our policy and as a consequence of our Agreement with China, this frontier should be considered a firm and definite one which is not open to discussion with anybody,' he added. On the other hand, China's official maps laid claims over Aksai Chin and Arunachal Pradesh.[24]

In 1958, India had officially stated that Aksai Chin was its territory.[25] Meanwhile, a rebellion was brewing in Tibet, where the Chinese Army began crushing the voices that were against the Communist Party of China. Tibetan spiritual leader Dalai Lama fled Tibet and was given a warm reception in India. The Indian government decided to give him asylum. The Dalai Lama formed the Tibetan government in-exile in India, but it changed the relationship and mutual understanding between

---

[23]Srinath Raghavan, 'Sino-Indian boundary dispute, 1948–60: A reappraisal,' *Economic and Political Weekly*, 41(36), 3882-3892, 2006, http://www.jstor.org/stable/4418679, accessed 18 May 2021.

[24]Prabhash K. Dutta, 'China-India war started with synchronised attack on Ladakh, Arunachal,' *India Today*, 20 October 2017, https://www.indiatoday.in/india/story/india-china-war-1962-20-october-aksai-chin-nefa-arunchal-pradesh-1067703-2017-10-20, accessed 16 June 2021.

[25]Srinath Raghavan,' Sino-Indian Boundary Dispute, 1948-60: A Reappraisal,' *Economic and Political Weekly*, Vol. 41, No. 36, 2006, pp. 3882–3892. JSTOR, www.jstor.org/stable/4418679, accessed 16 June 2021.

India and China to a great extent and the same year, Indian and Chinese forces clashed at several posts. But till the start of the war, the Indian side was confident that nothing of the sort could happen and made little preparations.

The Sino-Indian war officially began when the People's Liberation Army of China invaded Ladakh and Arunachal Pradesh (then known as the North-east Frontier Agency [NEFA]). Their invasion was well synchronized and the events took New Delhi by complete surprise.

Alarmed by the Chinese aggression and assertiveness, New Delhi decided to launch what it described as its Forward Policy in 1961. The objective of the policy was to create outposts behind advancing Chinese troops to cut supplies, thus forcing them to retreat to north of the demarcated lines. Deployments were made at several posts. However, skirmishes continued throughout the first half of 1962. The Chinese also cut Indian telephone lines, preventing the defenders from making contact with their headquarters. The biggest reason for India's failure in putting up a strong fight against the Chinese forces was that the Indian think tanks were not entirely convinced that China would go to war with India. There was not the slightest of anticipation among the diplomatic circles though the ties between the two neighbours had been rapidly deteriorating. It is also worth noting that the Chinese managed to outplay their Indian counterparts all through the war by holding on to their cards. They did not reveal their intentions while Indian troops were struggling to hold on to their posts. India was of the opinion that China would only engage in small skirmishes as it was not in a position to wage a full-fledged war! The Chinese forces, however, made rapid advancements into Indian territories as the Indian Army was ill-prepared, poorly equipped and short in supplies.

When Chinese troops were 15 km inside the Indian territory, Chinese premiere Zhou Enlai shot off a letter to Nehru.[26] He proposed a ceasefire and offered a negotiated settlement. China suggested that both India and China should disengage and withdraw their troops 20 km behind the present Line of Actual Control. Enlai proposed Chinese withdrawal in Arunachal Pradesh (NEFA) while suggesting that India and China should maintain status quo in Aksai Chin. But, Nehru rejected the proposals saying that the Chinese claim on Aksai Chin was illegal.[27]

The Indian parliament then passed a resolution to 'drive out the aggressors from the sacred soil of India'. With a three-week ceasefire, the war lasted till 21 November, when China unilaterally withdrew from Indian territories before snow could block safe passage to its forces. According to China's official military history, the war achieved China's policy objectives of securing borders in its western sector.[28] Around 3,250 Indian soldiers were killed. India lost about 43,000 sq. km of land, captured by China in Aksai Chin. While the bloody episode

---

[26]'Premier Chou En-Lai's [Zhou Enlai's] Letter to the Leaders of Asian and African Countries on the Sino-Indian Boundary Question (15 November 1962), Wilson Center, https://digitalarchive.wilsoncenter.org/document/175946.pdf?v =404219d0404b58d9d0eb299c55521da9, accessed 16 June 2021.
[27]Ibid.
[28]India Today Web Desk, 'India-China War of 1962: How it started and what happened later,' *India Today*, 21 November 2016, https://www. indiatoday.in/education-today/gk-current-affairs/story/india-china-war-of-1962-839077-2016-11-21, accessed 10 May 2021.

would be buried deep in memory, the territory India lost was almost the size of Switzerland and thousands of its courageous soldiers had sacrificed their lives in the line of battle.

The entire country was filled with grief; our fears were overpowering us. Would we lose our independence? The freedom that we often took for granted?

On the cold winter evening of 27 January 1963, the general sentiment of the country was expressed in a song to an audience of thousands in New Delhi. Its words became the guiding light and ushered hope, confidence and self-belief among the people during those troubled days when morale and esteem were low. As legendary singer Lata Mangeshkar put Kavi Pradeep's '*Ae mere watan ke logon* (O people of my country)' to her melody, many in the grieving nation found reasons to believe in the power of their will. The song that was going to trigger emotions of great patriotic pride brought tears to the eyes of Nehru.

There's a saying that there are lessons in defeat that victory can't teach. For India as an independent country, the lesson from the war was coming to terms with reality and to build its strengths while fixing its weaknesses. It was in knowing that it was not the only independent country in the world, in accepting that there would always be threats and in believing that it could empower the capabilities of its people with technological advancements and better universities. It was in questioning the diplomatic and political leadership, and in bringing the nation up to the times it was passing through. It was in striving to be better than ourselves.

The country was won over by the valour of its armed forces even though they were unquestionably ill-prepared. The people understood that the army showed extraordinary bravery in the face of unfavourable conditions and a formidable opponent at that point in time. It was a grateful nation paying tribute to its martyrs by promising to strengthen its weaknesses and being worthy of their sacrifice. The song that continues to evoke sentiments five decades later had also pointed to the values of unity.

The war reminded many of the sacrifices the soldiers made, as also of the courageous freedom fighters, such as Bhagat Singh, Sukhdev and Rajguru, and Netaji Subhas Chandra Bose and the Indian National Army, of whom there were only mentions in history textbooks. It made them value their freedom.

'O people of my country,' the song called. 'Let us shout the slogan, this auspicious day belongs to us all. But do not forget the brave soldiers who lost their lives on the border. Give a thought to those who didn't return home.' It went on to evoke memories of the war, reminding people that when the Himalayas were wounded and their freedom was threatened, the brave soldiers of their country fought till the very end.

It rightly encapsulated the mood of the country at that point in time. All Indians were united in defeat and shared grief. That moment perhaps helped India realize what it truly meant to be a country, a people who share a similar identity. It was thus that the song mentioned in detail the extraordinary virtue of Indian diversity and sought to point out its strength to the listeners.

Nehru wrote in *Discovery of India*:

India with all her infinite charm and variety began to grow upon me more and more, and yet the more I saw of her, the more I realized how very difficult it was for me or for

57

anyone else to grasp the ideas she had embodied. It was not her wide spaces that eluded me, or even her diversity, but some depth of soul which I could not fathom, though I had occasional and tantalizing glimpses of it. She was like some ancient palimpsest on which layer upon layer of thought and reverie had been inscribed, and yet no succeeding layer had completely hidden or erased what had been written previously. All of these existed in our conscious or subconscious selves, though we may not have been aware of them, and they had gone to build up the complex and mysterious personality of India. That sphinx-like face with its elusive and sometimes mocking smile was to be seen throughout the length and breadth of the land. Though outwardly there was diversity and infinite variety among our people, everywhere there was that tremendous impress of oneness, which had held all of us together for ages past, whatever political fate or misfortune had befallen us.[29]

But Nehru did not think of India, or any country for that matter, as what some may call 'an anthropomorphic entity'. He was fully aware of the diversities and divisions of Indian life, of classes, castes, religions, races as well as different degrees of cultural development.

Soldiers are patriots of a different kind. They are wild, protective, caring and are unwavering in their loyalty towards

[29]Jawaharlal Nehru, *The Discovery of India*, Centenary edition, Oxford University Press, Delhi, 1994, pp. 58–59, http://library.bjp.org:8080/jspui/bitstream/123456789/277/1/The-Discovery-Of-India-Jawaharlal-Nehru.pdf, accessed 1 June 2021.

their motherland. The highest price is their ultimate sacrifice and through rain and shine they seek to serve the interests of their countries. Regardless of whichever country they belong to, their people owe a great deal of gratitude to them for their services and selfless sacrifices. They lead a disciplined life, which is more tiring and devoid of comfort as compared to the ordinary citizens and are at their duties relentlessly, forsaking personal milestones, struggles and celebrations.

But while valour and courage may be the hallmarks of a soldier, it is not mandatorily expected of the people to deploy these in their day-to-day lives. They are also not mandatorily required to become warmongers or support war. Denouncing war is actually a more patriotic thing to do. But we should be aware that patriotism also demands protection of the patria, which in turn implies safeguarding and upholding the Indian Constitution. Similarly, it can sometimes be the case that an all-out war will find justification by patriots in the face of a threat to the sovereignty of India.

Wars, interestingly, are also times that are ripe for exploitation and the unthinking human heart realizes its folly perhaps when very little is left to be done. Rudyard Kipling, though not widely remembered as a war poet, saw a devastating effect of war on his own life.

With the First World War breaking out in 1914, Kipling, who was then already in his late forties, could not enlist in the army. But he vociferously used his writing to fuel the propaganda for Britain, crafting idealistic images of the armed forces. He is even credited with coining 'the Hun', which demonized the German enemy.[30] His writings, though jingoistic, were immensely popular. Soldiers were particularly fond of his verses. Kipling is said to have become adamant that his only son John (known as Jack) joined the army. He is even said to have secured his son's entry through his connections. But then it came back to haunt Kipling when John went missing in action during heavy machine gun fire in the battle of Loos in 1915. Kipling could never know what happened to his son and that shattered him.

In response to the dreadful sequence of events that had led to his son's disappearance in the war, Kipling wrote 'My Boy Jack'. Most believe that Kipling was referring to his own lost son.

'Have you news of my boy Jack?'
Not this tide.
'When d'you think that he'll come back?'
Not with this wind blowing, and this tide.

'Has anyone else had word of him?'
Not this tide.
For what is sunk will hardly swim,
Not with this wind blowing, and this tide.

'Oh, dear, what comfort can I find?'
None this tide,
Nor any tide,

---

[30]Ellie Cawthorne, '5 influential WW1 poets you should know about,' History Extra, 3 August 2020, https://www.historyextra.com/period/first-world-war/ww1-world-war-one-poets-wilfred-owen-hedd-wyn-siegfried-sassoon-rupert-brooke-rudyard-kipling-famous/, accessed 10 May 2021.

Except he did not shame his kind—
Not even with that wind blowing, and that tide.

Then hold your head up all the more,
This tide,
And every tide;
Because he was the son you bore,
And gave to that wind blowing and that tide!

Like the many complexities with life and everything else, mankind's response to war has been mixed. But if you look at it from the point of view of patriotism, then it is different in the sense that it has patriots on both sides of the border. Indian patriots on one side and Chinese patriots on the other. Patriots attacking patriots. Patriots killing patriots.

Think of it this way: the earth is so old but life is very recent in comparison; humans came later, and nations came much later. Now, we have reached a stage where we are sending missions to other planets and are yet so hell-bent on fighting wars. And patriotism is the fire that keeps the engine buzzing. But then, this entire exercise of nationhood that governs life on the fragile promise of safety nets is betrayed when a war is raged.

Far away from the grief of bloodshed and destructions unleashed by the war, life had quite a different meaning in Ayemenem, the beautiful village in Kerala that would later be immortalized in an award-winning novel. This is where young Susie came with her mother after she separated with her husband. Religion and caste systems had a great role in defining society. There were few wealthy people but many poor and deprived, movement among social groups was almost unimaginable and communism had a great pull for the poor. For young Susie, more than anything else, Meenachil river had a distinct pull. Formed by several streams originating from the Western Ghats, the river flows through the heart of the Kottayam district in Kerala and passes calmly through Ayemenem. Coconut trees bent towards the river as boats passed by. She was an unprotected child in a closed and parochial surrounding.

When she was barely five years old, Susannah learnt to sit still—silently in one position—for hours to catch fish. She could walk to the river bank at any time of the day; there was hardly anybody to stop her from doing so. As she trained herself to sit silently for long hours without a thought in her mind that could sway her attention, she gradually gained mastery over the art of concentration, minutely observing everything that caught her attention. The ability to concentrate in that country setting was incredible.

'My mother was very ill, she had left her husband, and one saw the vulnerability of that woman and then her anger would come out against us. And living there in the village, one saw the playing out of caste and all of that. The Lolitas of the world were my friends and I could see how the adult world was playing out before my eyes.'

There were no restaurants or cinema halls, no television and not even a telephone for young Susie to indulge in during her early days. Fortunately, the British Council library in Madras (now Chennai) used to send a set of hundred books every three months to her school. This was the 'high point' of her life and she would eagerly wait for the next set of books to arrive. She read Shakespeare and Kipling when she was very young and could recite monologues from *Julius Caesar* and *The Merchant of Venice* when most others of her age struggled to make sense of them.

Shashi was a voracious reader too, but he was also a goal setter.

'He wishes to pursue humanities,' complained his teachers. 'He is excellent at science, in fact, the best in his class.' Shashi's parents stood and listened on in silence. They had been summoned to the school after the then ninth-standard student expressed his decision to drop science as soon as he had an opportunity to. He was the star student of his school, the favourite of his many teachers and one they had a lot of expectations from. Therefore, when they suddenly found out that he was dropping science and opting for humanities instead, they thought they could still persuade the young man to study science.

But what came across as a sudden decision for his teachers was actually a natural calling, something that Shashi had been passionately involved in. Above all subjects, he loved literature and history. He recalls that these were two particular subjects where he was not only paying attention in class but was also reading much more than the teacher or the textbooks and syllabus required him to. He had his secret little notebook in which, although not required by the school, he would write many essays. 'Let's say I heard about the Black Hole of Calcutta (now Kolkata), I would go about researching it, look it up in libraries and then write my own essays on it. Somehow that fascination was there,' he says.

In fact, the St. Stephen's College admission committee was so surprised when he applied for history with such marks that he got admitted without an interview, which rarely happens at an institution of its repute. He came to Delhi University three months after his sixteenth birthday, it was an age when experiences had a lasting influence. He went to Kamala Nagar and sometimes beyond that, participated in quizzes and extempore and more, and also played Mark Antony to Mira Nair's *Cleopatra*. The presence of classmates, friends, seniors and juniors from every corner of the country, from every religion, every language and background gave Shashi his profound faith in India.

Quite to the contrary, the natural beauty surrounding the pristine village or little privileges that young Susie enjoyed as a child did not spare her from being exposed to caste segregation and she faced the brunt of the social evil first-hand. Just as the river pulsed through the darkness behind her, the many darker faces and cases of the mortal world made their appearance, one by one, or often, they ganged up together to the perils of young Susie. She was called 'Address illa' (meaning 'the one without an address') because, according to many in the village, she did not have an ancestral lineage.

She was exposed to the vitriol of social inequality in her childhood and therefore her inclinations would shift in a very profound manner. Her world could not be measured in statistics and numbers that run on screens, her thoughts ran really deep, as there was no safety net of any sort protecting her from the ferocity, the ugliness and the unexpected blows of the outside world.

When an outward and mythological sense of the patria, Bharat Mata, creeps into our imagination and serving it blindly becomes the goal of our subconscious mind, we stop understanding why we feel patriotic in the first place.

We feel patriotic when we believe that the governments

that are ruling us will protect us and safeguard our interests. We may also feel patriotic if we have a sense of historical and cultural attachment to the patria. When things are the way they are in modern nations, historical and cultural pretexts to patriotism aren't something totally unheard of. The word 'patria' itself arose from Rome.

So, many people with historical or cultural lineage are often patriotic, but it all boils down to how they understand or view the patria. Patriotism denotes one's sense of attachment to the patria and the Constitution is the manifestation of that bond in a liberal democracy such as India. But how would you apply that in a nation where thousands can't even read or write their names, let alone understand their rights and constitutional guarantees? The failure in curbing exploitation and injustice from society is the bitter reality against which a gulf has continuously built between our people and the patria. It is not something that you can poke and arouse; it is a sense we acquire.

There is something very profound in the being of the nation, in the shared holidays and postal stamps, that we become members of the tribe, so to say. We may take pride in some aspects of our history and not so much in others, but most of us ultimately find comfort in the sense of home and that is just one of the things that shape our understanding of patriotism. Now, people would not feel patriotic when their country isn't exhibiting the behaviour they expect, or perhaps when they are being outright cruel, xenophobic and increasingly self-centred and greedy, or when they find that the governments and the corporations do not care anymore, that they are just there, the faces we see to hide the powers that be. People may also feel less and less patriotic when they realize that they are not loved by their fellow countrymen. The more oppression there is, the more are the threats to patriotism.

So, the choice really is like picking what kind of a world you would want to live in rather than what kind of a world you come from. And let's say, you identify yourself as a patriot, but that doesn't mean that you are the only patriot in the land and that all patriots should necessarily agree with you. In fact, patriotism may mean very different things to different people. The Indian freedom movement, for instance, is the source of inspiration for most who identify themselves as patriots in India. But the freedom movement is not a singular story; it wasn't something that was fought and achieved overnight. It took years of struggle and numerous sacrifices by many to attain freedom from the British empire and even then, the methods applied by our freedom fighters were different from each other.

The word 'Indian' means different things to different people, but it also evokes some similar sentiments. It is the feeling of a common identity, it is the testimony of where we come from and it is the reminder of the promise we made to those who laid their lives to secure our freedom. These are all feelings associated with nationhood and patriotism and most of us can relate to these images.

But what does it really mean to be patriotic? Independence Day, Republic Day, Gandhi Jayanti—are these mere holidays in the national calendar? They are to keep us grounded and to help us reflect on the sacrifices made by the men and women who have gone before us. On such occasions, Indians join hands and remember the freedom fighters who stood against the British and seek to build for themselves the kinds of lives and society that they hope and aspire for. These are moments for us to honour those who have done so much for our nation. India wasn't a superpower during this time. It had, in fact, just lost a major war, but people were proud to be Indians even though they were going through one of the nation's toughest times.

It was in times like these that patriotism was tested. It can also be seen as the collective resolve of the people to affirm their identity. In a country like India, with deeply divided views and beliefs of patriotism, several people may also not consider themselves patriotic. They may find that patriotism as it exists in our society is nothing but another form of blind nationalism. It may even seem terrifying to them. There is another significant trend to note and that is the rationale that has shaped the understanding of patriotism in a manner that involves hoisting and waving flags and hailing the military. While people may actually believe in the strength of their army, they may also find that these are empty acts. People may find these to be just outward symbols and while these may be significant in the historical and political trajectory of their nations, there are also other things that actually make their countries more impressive.

At the end of the war with China, for example, people were won over by the valour of the Indian armed forces. But would that make somebody who questioned the army and political leadership for their failure during the war any less patriotic?

It was hardly the case. The political and military leadership came under immense fire. They were questioned for India's poor performance in the war, the lack of its preparedness and its failure in ensuring the safety of the country's borders. India's defeat in the war came to be seen from two major perspectives.

The primary reason for the defeat was evaluated as the diplomatic failure of the Nehru administration to arrive at a solution with China.[31] And the strategic folly of engaging in a 'forward policy' that could not be supplied properly with food, equipment, and arms and ammunition also came under the scanner. So, one thing that emerged quite clearly in this hour of grief, when hearts were most solemn, was simply the fact that the people were one as a country and that they wanted to overcome their errors and secure their future. That was the meaning of being patriotic, to have faith and hold on to the common thread while also contributing their bit for the common good.

Shashi came to Delhi University three months after his sixteenth birthday and would leave it shortly after his nineteenth. It is an impressionable age and he says that of his entire life in campus, the classrooms were perhaps the least important aspect, before going on to talk at length about the extracurricular activities he actively participated in and his involvement in everything from reviving the Wodehouse society to starting the Quiz Club, and acting in plays with the Shakespeare society. The young lad now had newer and exciting aspirations. He wanted to travel abroad and study at an internationally renowned institution. Shashi's plan was to complete his master's degree and then appear for the Indian Foreign Service examinations, and hopefully obtain a good job in foreign services to settle for life. It was this quest that led him

---

[31]Siddharth Singh, '1962 war debacle—the errors Jawaharlal Nehru made,' *Mint*, 19 March 2014, https://www.livemint.com/Opinion/HCs4SMg2ojRh1T024T1KxO/1962-war-debaclethe-errors-Jawaharlal-Nehru-made.html, accessed 10 May 2021.

to explore various options even before he was formally done with his undergraduate studies at St. Stephens College in New Delhi. But he was from a middle-class family and affording Shashi's stay and education abroad was not something his family could think of at that point of time. A scholarship was the need of the hour and he was well aware of this. No sooner had he decided that he was going to travel abroad for further studies that he began applying for scholarships. During those days, he recalls, if an applicant wished to pursue a master's course in the UK, he was required to have an undergraduate degree in hand at the time of application. Courses in the American universities, on the other hand, allowed candidates to apply for their courses while they were in the final year of their undergraduate studies. So, Shashi thought that it would be a better option to apply for the US because that would save him a year's time.

He says he applied to half a dozen universities and got admitted into all of them, but only two or three of them offered him scholarships. A partial scholarship was of little value to him as the amount that would still be required to afford his tenure abroad was too much for a middle-class Indian family to cough up. He was looking for a full scholarship and that came from Fletcher School of Law and Diplomacy, which offered him admission and full scholarship for a course that he was genuinely interested in—international affairs.

'Growing up in India, I had very little access to world events. Newspapers were just eight to 10 pages long and there would be only one page of world news. I remember devouring global news with great interest. I was extremely curious about what was going on elsewhere. So, when I got this scholarship from

Fletcher School of Law and Diplomacy to study international affairs, I said great, let's do it,' he recalls.

Shortly after his nineteenth birthday, Shashi, a young Indian in the emerging era of globalization, left for the US.

5

Stop! It's Emergency

P eople living in a particular geographical area who adhere to a common set of laws are generally perceived as the citizens of a given country. In India's case, as we explored at length in the previous chapters, most rules were formulated in Britain and it was only after Independence that the Constitution of India came into force. Among the outcomes of the fall of the British empire, particularly significant was the fact that India became a democratic republic, where people governed themselves through their elected representatives.

However, patriotism holds significance in democracies too and because power is vested with the people in such a form of government, they are sometimes expected to remain vigilant and ensure that the governments ruling them do not become autocratic or authoritative in their behaviour.

Therefore, just like the army has a role to play in securing the safety of the country, the common citizens too are faced with moments when they are driven by patriotism to safeguard the values on which their countries are founded. A country is not a mere geographical entity; it is the coexistence of its people and the laws they adopted to govern themselves. An imbalance between the two usually results in turmoil. These do not happen every day, but threats to democracies have surfaced in several forms in different countries from time to time, as it happened in India during the mid 1970s.

Nehru had single-handedly dominated India's political establishment for nearly 17 years after Independence. He remained the indisputable leader till the time of his death in 1964 and most of his contemporaries were overshadowed by his towering persona. On 27 May 1964, Nehru breathed his last. He was 74.

Nehru's demise was expected to throw up a power struggle among senior Congress leaders, but the situation was avoided as Lal Bahadur Shastri was unanimously elected to lead the country. This symbolic and peaceful transition symbolized India's commitment to democracy and its growing maturity on the global stage.

Becoming the prime minister of India at a time when many parts of the country were faced with severe drought and famine-like situations, Shastri laid great emphasis on the White and Green revolutions.[32] Such policies helped usher India in the path of self-reliance and development. It is also important to

---

[32]Mihir Bose, '1960's: India's changing phase,' *India Today*, 30 November 1999, https://www.indiatoday.in/magazine/india-today-archives/story/20070702-indian-decade-of-dos-and-donts-1960s-748418-1999-11-30, accessed 11 May 2021.

note that tremendous importance and priority was given to strengthening the capabilities of the Indian army following the debacle of the 1962 war with China. The nation came together in the aftermath of defeat and paid glowing tributes to its martyrs while the political establishment understood the importance of modernizing the military.

While hippie culture and civil rights movements were gaining ground in the western part of the world, India's immediate focus was consolidating its military and safeguarding its sovereign interests as an independent nation. Leading film stars of the time, such as Dilip Kumar and Nargis Dutt, were also holding events for raising funds for the armed forces.[33] These were times when writers such as V.S. Naipaul and Nirad C. Chaudhuri had come out with books such as *An Area of Darkness*[34] and *The Continent of Circe*[35], respectively, which were pessimistic in their outlook.

But then, in 1966, Shastri went to Tashkent in the then Union of Soviet Socialist Republics (USSR) to sign a peace accord with Pakistan. He died there under mysterious circumstances, which have been a subject of rigorous investigation by several scholars since then. A void was once again created at the very top of the nation's governance and this time, Nehru's daughter,

---

[33]Rasheed Kidwai, 'Indian politics has a long history of seeking help from Bollywood,' *Quartz India*, 13 November 2018, https://qz.com/india/1460002/how-nehru-modi-used-bollywood-stars-in-indian-politics/, accessed 11 May 2021.

[34]V.S. Naipaul, *An Area of Darkness: His Discovery of India*, Picador; Main Market edition, 2012.

[35]Nirad C. Chaudhuri, *The Continent of Circe: Essays on the People of India*, Jaico Publishing House; 17th Impression edition, 1999.

Indira Gandhi, was pushed forward by senior members of the Congress party as they thought they could rule by proxy through her as she was expected to behave like a *goongi gudiya* (dumb doll),[36] though she would prove the sceptics wrong.

We should remember that in 1950, India became a republic, which meant that it would not be ruled by a hereditary monarch. Mrs Gandhi's ascent to the top, though through democratic means, challenged that essential feature and would emerge as a reason of contentious debate several generations down the line. While India had so far been governed largely by one party, her rise to power would change it into one woman for several years, and what many argue, one family, thereafter.

Mrs Gandhi is said to have acquired the basics of diplomacy since her early days as she accompanied her father during his official trips and visits. She engaged with world leaders as well as leaders at the grassroots from quite a young age. She would routinely welcome diplomats and international politicians home in India and also travel with her father to major conferences across the country and the world too.[37] Having joined the Congress formally in 1955, she became its president barely four years later. So, it wasn't like she was completely unknown when she became the prime minister. Her rise is generally attributed to two primary factors. First, the single-party dominance of the Congress was losing ground

[36]Kuldeep Nayar, 'Remembering Indira Gandhi on her 35th death anniversary,' *The Telegraph Online*, 31 October 2019, https://www.telegraphindia.com/culture/remembering-indira-gandhi-on-her-35th-death-anniversary/cid/1715657, accessed 11 May 2021.
[37]History editors, 'Indira Gandhi,' History.com, 10 June 2019, https://www.history.com/topics/india/indira-gandhi, accessed 11 May 2021.

after Nehru's demise and apparently, there was a crisis of food supplies, which was turning more and more people against the ruling establishment. Second, many thought that Mrs Gandhi could be influenced and moulded easily.

As the daughter of India's first prime minister, she was expected to win votes for the Congress and ensure that it remained in power.[38] But she proved them wrong with her tenacity and gained control over the government.[39]

Soon, there was an attempt to oust her from the Congress party. But she turned the table on the elites by removing her key opponent Morarji Desai from the post of finance minister and brought the ministry under her control.[40] And then she enacted pro-people policies such as nationalization of banks and devaluation of the Indian rupee.[41] These not only helped India sail through a rough phase, when it managed to avert famine and bankruptcy but also cemented her persona among the masses. Her popularity soared, and she was grabbing more and more power with every passing day.

---

[38]Prabhash K. Dutta, 'Indira Gandhi, a goongi gudiya who went on to become Iron Lady,' *India Today*, 19 November 2017, https://www.indiatoday.in/india/story/indira-gandhi-a-goongi-gudiya-who-went-on-to-become-iron-lady-1089668-2017-11-19, accessed 11 May 2021.

[39]Bipan Chandra, Aditya Mukherjee and Mridula Mukherjee, *India since Independence, the Indira Gandhi years*, Penguin Books, 2008.

[40]Shantanu Gupta, 'Indira Gandhi vs Morarji Desai: How JNU was at the centre of battle to capture academia,' *The Print*, 17 January 2020, https://theprint.in/pageturner/excerpt/indira-gandhi-vs-morarji-desai-how-jnu-was-at-the-centre-of-battle-to-capture-academia/350831/, accessed 11 May 2021.

[41]Amol Agarwal, 'Why Indira Gandhi nationalised India's banks,' BloombergQuint, 12 July 2019, https://www.bloombergquint.com/opinion/why-indira-gandhi-nationalised-indias-banks, accessed 11 May 2021.

Things became worse after the death of the then president Zakir Husain in 1969, when the Congress nominated N. Sanjeeva Reddy as the presidential candidate against her wishes, but Mrs Gandhi did not issue a whip to her party members. Instead, she asked the Congress legislators to vote according to their conscience.[42] As it emerged, almost one-third of her party members did not vote for Reddy but instead chose an independent candidate, V.V. Giri, who became the vice president of India. Following this, she was expelled from the party.[43] She set up a rival organization and most Congress members of parliament (MPs) stood by her.

As elections approached in 1971, Mrs Gandhi rode to power once again, but a conflict surfaced between East and West Pakistan. She played a crucial role in the creation of Bangladesh and soon came to be known as the 'Iron Lady of India'. Her tactics were acknowledged internationally too. Having learnt its lessons from the blunders it made against China in 1962, India coordinated well between the activities of its army, the Border Security Force and intelligence units.[44] Mrs Gandhi was slowly assuming power and support in proportions that nobody had enjoyed in India so far. Her building clout was further elevated

---

[42]'1969: S. Nijalingappa expelled Indira Gandhi from the party,' *India Today*, 8 April 2011, https://www.indiatoday.in/magazine/cover-story/story/20070702-1969-congress-splits-748296-2007-07-02, accessed 11 May 2021.

[43]Robert L. Hardgrave, 'The Congress in India: Crisis and Split,' *Asian Survey*, Vol. 10, No. 3, 1970, pp. 256–262. JSTOR, www.jstor.org/stable/2642578, accessed 16 June 2021.

[44]'How Indira Gandhi pulled off India's victory against Pakistan during 1971 Bangladesh Liberation War,' News 18 India, https://www.news18.com/news/india/indira-gandhi-102nd-birth-anniversary-india-s-role-in-1971-india-pakistan-bangladesh-liberation-war-2391829.html, accessed 11 May 2021.

after the liberation of Bangladesh, but just as she was emerging as the most powerful leader in the history of independent India, Mrs Gandhi was also acquiring a cult status of sorts among the people. As Ranbir Vohra noted in *The Making of India: A Political History*[45], she began to show signs of authoritarianism and became intolerant towards criticism.

And that's when dissent perhaps became an arm of patriotism in independent India.

With Mrs Gandhi's rise, her political opponents could gauge the impact of the uncontrollable and unchallengeable powers that she came to control. You see, the republic of India was founded on some basic principles, as we discussed in Chapter 3. Freedom, rights and a democratic set-up were central to the way in which we had decided to govern ourselves. At the same time, it was also important to prevent centralization of power in the hands of one person.[46] But these were challenged under what many criticized as authoritative behaviour. So, the very promise of freedom upon which the Indian freedom movement was built had turned out to be a betrayal of sorts as a leader had risen to the top with popular public support and was now unwilling to respect that solemn bond.[47]

In 1973, a mass agitation surfaced in Gujarat over rising

---

[45]Ranbir Vohra, *The Making of India: A Political History*, Routledge; 3rd edition, 2012.

[46]B. Chandra, *In the name of democracy: JP Movement and the Emergency*, India: Random House Publishers India Pvt. Limited, 2017.

[47]Srinivas Mazumdaru, 'Indira Gandhi: India's democrat with an authoritarian bent,' DW, 19 November 2017, https://www.dw.com/en/indira-gandhi-indias-democrat-with-an-authoritarian-bent/a-41427087, accessed 16 June 2021.

prices and shortage of food materials.[48] Long serpentine queues for basic commodities were a regular site in the state during those days. The state assembly was dissolved, but when elections took place two years later, an alliance of opposition parties defeated the Congress and gave Mrs Gandhi a taste of democracy. At the same time, another popular mass leader Jayaprakash Narayan (JP) called for 'total revolution' and fuelled a massive movement that began in Bihar. With the rising tide of 'Sampoorna Kranti', JP emerged as the key opponent to Mrs Gandhi's authoritarian regime[49] and it became one of the most remarkable moments in the history of India. The people at large were extremely poor, as a lot of India's wealth was being invested in security and in laying the foundations of long-term projects. Their anger against starvation and the lack of food supplies combined with their fears of losing democracy built up as a people's movement against Mrs Gandhi.

JP stressed that power should return to people and that youth should become the agents of change.[50] And that is exactly how things played out in India. After the Nav Nirman Andolan in Gujarat, he mobilized the youth in Bihar to fight corruption

---

[48]Dr Jhumur Ghosh, 'Indira Gandhi's call of Emergency and press censorship in India: The ethical parameters revisited,' *Global Media Journal* – Indian Edition, ISSN 2249 – 5835; Winter-Summer Issue/December 2016–June 2017; Volume: 7/Number: 2, Volume: 8/Number: 1.

[49]'Authoritarian India,' *The New York Times*, https://www.nytimes.com/1975/12/31/archives/authoritarian-india.html, accessed 16 June 2021.

[50]ET Bureau, 'Jayaprakash Narayan: The saintly leader & crusader for clean polity,' *The Economic Times*, 11 October 2018, https://economictimes.indiatimes.com/news/politics-and-nation/jayaprakash-narayan-the-saintly-leader-crusader-for-clean-polity/articleshow/66157358.cms?from=mdr, accessed 11 May 2021.

and authoritarianism. He maintained, as Bipan Chandra noted in *In the Name of Democracy: JP Movement and the Emergency*[51], that Mrs Gandhi in the prime minister's post was incompatible with the survival of democracy in India.

It almost seemed that an electoral confrontation between her and JP was approaching even though the former always maintained that power was not her aim. However, a crucial court ruling in 1975 resulted in the sudden breakdown of democratic principles. While hearing a petition of electoral malpractices, Justice Jagmohanlal Sinha of the Allahabad High Court convicted Mrs Gandhi for indulging in corrupt campaigning practices in the parliamentary elections of 1971. He further declared her election null and void. It meant that she could no longer hold on to the office of prime minister.

This happened at a time when there was already a nationwide angst against Mrs Gandhi since JP's movement had gained ground and a large number of students got involved with it. JP accused her of occupying an office that she had gained corruptly and demanded her immediate resignation. A civil disobedience movement took shape as key leaders of the time urged the people to disobey the orders and put hurdles in the way of government functions. Leaders were also urging police personnel, the army and bureaucrats to refuse to obey government order.

'The respondent no. I (Indira Gandhi) was thus guilty of a corrupt practice under Section 123(7) of the Act...accordingly stands disqualified for a period of six years from the date of

---

[51]B. Chandra, *In the name of democracy: JP Movement and the Emergency*, India: Random House Publishers India Pvt. Limited, 2017.

this order...' Justice Sinha pronounced.[52] Mrs Gandhi, present in person in the court, was left dumbstruck. It is important to note that on an appeal filed by her, the Supreme Court granted a conditional stay on Justice Sinha's verdict allowing her to continue as the prime minister, but she was debarred from taking part in parliamentary proceedings and drawing salary as an MP. But instead of respecting the verdict of the court, Mrs Gandhi plunged India into what turned out to be the darkest hours of its democratic life by imposing Emergency and suspending all fundamental rights.

Late Kuldip Nayar, the veteran journalist who lived through those troubled days, later recalled:

> After the Allahabad judgement, Indira had thought of stepping down. I believe that if she had done so and had gone back to the people for a verdict on her electoral offence, offering her apologies, she would have got re-elected. However, two persons dissuaded her from doing so. One was her principal adviser and son, Sanjay Gandhi, who completely ruled out her resignation. The other was Siddhartha Shankar Ray, then the West Bengal chief minister, who advised her to impose an Emergency. She reportedly told him that India was already under an Emergency following the Bangladesh war. He said what he meant was an internal Emergency which would enable her to suspend fundamental rights and allow her to rule

---

[52]Satya Prakash, 'The court verdict that prompted Indira Gandhi to declare Emergency,' *Hindustan Times*, 26 June 2015, https://www.hindustantimes.com/india/the-court-verdict-that-prompted-indira-gandhi-to-declare-emergency/story-uaDsy0j3B0vSdiPn2md9WO.html, accessed 11 May 2021.

as she wished. Instead of appealing against the judgement, Indira Gandhi imposed a state of Emergency, including strict censorship and detaining her most feared political adversaries.[53]

Officially issued by President Fakhruddin Ali Ahmed under Article 352 of the Constitution, Mrs Gandhi sought to justify the Emergency on the grounds that the disruptions caused by the JP movement were threats to the integrity, stability and security of India.[54] She accused the opposition leaders of inciting rebellion and reached out to the people stating that she wished to usher a rapid economic development programme for the underprivileged. Journalists like Nayar were detained while the freedom of press was subjugated and people's liberties were snatched amid widespread reports of human rights violations.[55]

We seldom pause to think what patriotism would mean to people in such moments in their nation's history. Imagine, people go about their day-to-day lives, but all of a sudden something so big happens that it changes the very relationship they share with the world around them. The government had been elected by the people. Its duty was to serve them in humility and to acknowledge that the people must have the freedom to express their dissent or demand better of them.

---

[53]Kuldip Nayar, *On leaders and icons: From Jinnah to Modi*, Speaking Tiger, 2019.
[54]'Speech and Proclamation,' *The New York Times*, https://www.nytimes.com/1975/06/27/archives/speech-and-proclamation.html, accessed 16 June 2021.
[55]William Borders, 'India Arrests One of Her Most Important Journalists,' *The New York Times*, https://www.nytimes.com/1975/07/26/archives/india-arrests-one-of-her-most-important-journalists.html, accessed 16 June 2021.

It was also important that the government and the elected representatives regarded the fact that they could be made to vacate their honourable positions in accordance with the laws laid down in the same Constitution that propelled them to power. The power to rule the country was not permanent; it was a contract struck down by the courts, but the arrogant leader had decided to rally against the people.

These things began unfolding in India barely months after Shashi had gone to the US. He was full of hopes and aspirations, writing short stories and articles for magazines and newspapers alongside his studies.

Shashi's ambition up till this point in time was to obtain a master's degree and appear for the IFS examinations. But he would never appear for them. The horrific stories that emerged from India under the Emergency came across as very disillusioning to Shashi.

'Emergency was declared in 1975 and that was the time when I had just gone to the US. Like all good Indians, I initially defended my country and talked about why the Emergency was necessary and, in conversations with friends and professors, defended Indira Gandhi. But I had a roommate who was a journalist and he started coming with lots of news materials, telexes and so on. He brought me a huge amount of information from news agencies very little of which actually made it to the American papers. And I was reading a lot of very disturbing stuff about forced sterilization, media censorship, very disappointing things that had gone wrong during the Emergency. On top of that, I still remember the episode of a student leader from the University of Chicago who spoke out against the Emergency and the government. When the time came for his passport renewal, they refused to renew it. I had grown up taking my freedom and pride as an Indian citizen for granted and if my government could do something like this, how could I serve it? So, I never wrote the exam and instead went ahead with my PhD,' he recalls.

Back home in India, acclaimed novelist and Mrs Gandhi's cousin Nayantara Sahgal became a vehement opponent of the Emergency. She criticized the curbing of dissent and resigned from the Sahitya Akademi's Advisory Board for English.[56] In her resignation letter addressed to Dr R.S. Kelkar, the then secretary of the Akademi, Nayantara wrote that the question of free expression and free circulation of ideas is crucial to a free society. On the other hand, hundreds of people were being arrested and detained, and they were being punished for performing their patriotic duty.

JP is regarded as a patriot by most Indians today and he castigated Mrs Gandhi's actions in the strongest of words. While condemning the arrest of demonstrators and dissenters, he stressed upon her the importance of civil disobedience and unequivocally asked her to vacate the seat of prime minister. Patriotism was clearly the driving force during the days of Emergency as it was the case during the freedom struggle. It also turned out to be symbolic in the sense that the people, like JP, were fighting back to stake their claim in the patria by reminding the prime minister that they were opposed to her autocratic behaviour.

---

[56]Ritu Menon, 'Nayantara Sahgal's battle with Indira Gandhi,' *The Caravan*, 1 June 2014, https://caravanmagazine.in/essay/voice-dissent, accessed 16 June 2021.

So, opposing the government of the day does not necessarily mean or imply that the one opposing it is not a patriot. At the same time, supporting the government also doesn't change one's positions around patriotism. Consider the soldiers, for example. Even during those days of Emergency when most of their fellow countrymen were subjected to humiliation and were stripped of their rights, they remained vigilant at the borders with the same zeal and courage. Nothing deterred their spirits, but nothing could really demolish JP's resolve too.

In any diverse society, there is bound to be differences in terms of opinions, perceptions and prejudices, but patriotism naturally demands that people overcome such differences among them. Patriotism transcends such borders. The teacher does his job, the military serves their duties and citizens go about their usual business. Everybody has a part to play in keeping this ball rolling though we quite get carried away by our individualistic identities and symbolisms. Mrs Gandhi was overcome by the fear of losing power, so she took the patriotism of the people of India for granted. It was astonishing of her, Nehru's daughter of all people, to have taken that step and then carried on with repressive agendas. The actions of the government were not expected to cause anger and fear among people as freedom is something we often take for granted. We do not quite realize what its meaning is unless we are suddenly stripped of it. The anger that oozes out of us then takes the shape of patriotism.

Many student leaders during the Emergency became revolutionaries, confronting and clashing with the police and being detained and imprisoned for months. Most Indians, most certainly, didn't regard them as anti-nationals or traitors just because they were opposed to the authoritative attitude of

Mrs Gandhi's regime. On the contrary, we regard their acts as patriotic because they dared to speak up, and they mustered the courage to speak truth to power.

It is quite fascinating actually to note that patriotism is not something that comes alive only during the times of wars but is actually stitched into the fabric of our lives. Willingly or unwillingly, we are routinely made to remember our relationship with the patria. From our passports to vehicle registration numbers, everything that we see or hear around us is in some way related to the patria. The safety and well-being of the patria denote our safety, or so we think, which is why we take pride in our armies and celebrate stories that hail their sacrifices. But all of this happens because people have a sense of belongingness towards the patria and when something as disastrous as the Emergency takes place, that trust is broken.

The Emergency also stood to remind us of the dangers that the rise of authoritarianism can cause. It happened, and it could happen again. So, preventing it from happening also becomes a token of patriotism, which makes dissent so crucial to India after the Emergency. Though India had become independent in 1947, its people had not really found a voice. They remained quiet and struggled with their lives as wars were fought and devastating stories were lived all around them. The Emergency came at a tipping point when the people had already lost their cool over shortage of food items and the student uprising against the regime. The people became helpless while a government they elected absorbed absolute power. This wasn't the freedom that Gandhi and Bose fought for, this wasn't the fulfilment of the promises we made to ourselves and something needed to be done. Those who could fight, fought and those who could speak, spoke up. They took great pride in doing it, but as we recall their heroic acts, we should also remind ourselves that we too need to be vigilant. We need to constantly remind ourselves that our patriotism is not something that we blindly surrender in the hero-worship of any given leader, but it instead is the manifestation of our dreams and aspirations.

In many ways, patriotism denotes the way of life we want to lead. We take up issues and work for social causes, believing that they will make our world a better place, that every single drop counts and that every individual can make a difference. The extraordinary feature of the resentment against Mrs Gandhi's autocratic behaviour was the fact that the people overcame differences such as caste and religion. It was the fulfilment of unity, the realization of the power that the people have, which helped drive a patriotic fervour that was anti-establishment in its core belief. The government is not supposed to become the colonizer, though the lust and greed for power is such that it is often construed that way. Patriotism and dissent, therefore, went hand in hand during the Emergency and the years that followed saw a greater intellectual debate in the country when the crucial period would be evaluated again and again.

The Emergency was also a lesson for Indians, a reminder that their patriotism could be exploited to build an autocratic regime. In retrospect, there were ample signals of Mrs Gandhi's growing clout and many could, in fact, assess the implications of her rise well before she took the decision to impose it. Patriotism played defining roles in the sense that it was crucial in both the rise and fall of Mrs Gandhi. If people were swayed by her leadership during the Bangladesh liberation war, their angst also became evident as her policies turned repressive.

When people rose against Mrs Gandhi, it was a manifestation of patriotism because the people who came forward, at grave risks to themselves, did so because they had not imagined to be living in the India as it was during the times of Emergency. Times like these were also crucial in understanding the place of the patria in our lives.

It is a common belief in most parts of the world that the country we belong to is something we should be proud of and therefore singing of the national anthems and hoisting of national flags are gala occasions. But amid these outward displays, we should also understand that the people who owe the allegiance to these flags and songs are actually the ones who give them their authority and meaning. Therefore, the flags can be high only as long as the morale of the people are high and there will be little meaning in singing the national anthem when the people are actually unhappy and fearful in their day-to-day lives. It may give a sense of comfort for the time being, but even that shallow promise is broken when people realize that the governments ruling them are the ones curbing their freedoms.

The Emergency was a betrayal of freedom. Imagine living under suppression, when your freedoms are curbed, when newspapers are prevented from writing what should be written, when journalists are jailed and suppressed for voicing their opinion, when dissent is frowned upon and when everybody is expected to obey the diktats of the powers that be. Imagine the times when the security and law-enforcing agencies become the most dreadful enemies of the peoples' liberties and their rights let it be. What would patriotism mean at such junctures? Would patriotism have any meaning when those elected to govern the country are hell-bent on exploiting it? As India became Indira Gandhi and Indira Gandhi became India, the fine line between the nation and the post of the prime minister was diminished. Her orders were expected to be obeyed as patriotic duties of the citizens and those who disregarded them did so at their own peril.

And yet, there was such a huge show of dissent against her. People came out in thousands on the streets, students led the movements and even some newspapers showed exceptional courage during those daunting days. These were actions that were not just spontaneous but also natural. Feeling patriotic implies the sense of belongingness towards the country one lives in, but the country is made by the people and the rules that govern them. It is not a mere geographical identity. These rules are something that we make for ourselves and because we make these rules for ourselves, we make a democratic country. We did not make it a dictatorship or monarchy. We did not believe that a country of so many faiths and beliefs should be governed at the whims and fancies of one person, nor did we want the freedoms of the people to be curbed. Which is why patriotism means standing up for India, it means defending its constitutional values and fighting to prevent it from becoming tyranny.

It taught us lessons: that our feeling of goodwill can be exploited, that governments can become power hungry, that people can be let down and that their freedom can be threatened. These are not only external threats or the colonization of mere geographical landscape, but the possibility that even the governments that they elect can misuse that power to rob the people of their rights while demanding silence in return as their duties. There is a clash because when one feels patriotic, it is not merely about revelling in the Himalayas and the Ganges, though they may charm one in the same measure. It is also about the way of life, the freedoms, the responsibilities and mutual harmony.

6

Jingoism.com

Patriotism has been instrumental in the making of independent India and in ensuring the safety and security of the people while fulfilling the promise of independence through rights and liberties. It appears to be a very optimistic idea for the people, one that empowers them to make the best out of their lives in the larger course of the nation. At the same time, it is also something that helps in nation-building, in the country's integration and in fostering unity.

But it can also be a double-edged sword. Take a glass, for example, and fill it with water until you can fill no more. It will reach a saturation point and spill over. Patriotism can be used as a ploy, as a political weapon, in a manner that it longer represents its original self but instead begins acquiring traits and features that are, on the contrary, detrimental to the cause of the patria.

Let us first look at some basic aspects of patriotism as it evolved in India:

1. As we saw during the Indian freedom movement, the fostering of patriotism demands unity. The coming together of the people creates a buzz of sorts that helps fuel the patriotic waves in forms such as valour, sacrifice and martyrdom.

2. Patriotism, then, is about the nation, and about doing our bit for the common good. The nation, however, is defined in terms of the laws laid down in the Constitution, which becomes the ethos and values on which the foundations of the nation is laid.

3. We should also remember that patriotism in India did not mean only beating our chests; it was also about standing by our fellow countrymen in times of grief and defeat. It was about believing that we shall overcome, it was about holding on to each other.

4. There was, at the same time, a very clear and conscious attempt to overcome the burdens of the past and to build a society that was free from religious tensions. The idea of the patria was in a way above the idea of religion. One's religious identity didn't determine whether he was patriotic or not because the Constitution adopted by 'We the People' spelled out our desires to govern ourselves in a secular and democratic republic.

5. And still, if we could just look a little away, we could spot people going about their lives without the slightest realization or thought about patriotism. That was perhaps the beauty of it all because, what else would we

wish to achieve as the ultimate objectives of patriotism if not the well-being of the people and their harmony?

6. There were hurdles, of course. But there was also a desire to transform the constitutional guarantees into ground realities. There was suffering, starvation, corruption and hunger, but there was also a desire to overcome them.

7. Patriotism also meant remaining conscious that the power must remain with the people. It meant believing that aggressors and colonizers are not only outsiders, but the lust and greed to acquire absolute power may give way to fascist tendencies among politicians too.

Let us make it clear right at the outset that the Indian republic never attained its perfect self, the vision that it was founded upon. There were many hurdles, imperfections and challenges, but the successive regimes not only exploited its vulnerabilities to meet their political interests but also allowed the nation to gradually become something that it had not set out to be. The promise of equality remained a mere promise, while social justice was still a far-fetched dream. Patriotism was the most potent weapon that could enable Indians to reclaim their rights, but life is not a fairy tale. We have earlier noted in detail that there are two things that patriotism is inherently different from: religion and nationalism. But the rise of religious nationalism that sought supremacy on religious grounds gradually took the shape of jingoism in the Indian life.

Jingoism can broadly be identified as an extreme form of patriotism. But it is more than blind hero-worshipping of politicians or chanting of anthems. Jingoism exploits the vulnerabilities of patriotism. The things that make people insecure and the things they want to overcome and repair are what jingoists exploit in the name of patriotism.

Just like patriotism emerged as the natural inclination of people who were suppressed under the tyranny of the *Angrez*, jingoism too acquired its shape through constant contestation of history and a radical consolidation of communal sentiments. Difference in views regarding the way in which India should be governed after Independence had emerged during the course of the freedom movement. The Partition was an even greater blow to the nation and it led to further division along religious lines though there were efforts made by the State to restore communal harmony. Gandhi's assassination plunged the nation into grief, but then it also symbolized the existence of a parallel ideology. The Constitution of India was originally meant to settle that debate by spelling out our way of life thereafter. But even then, the glorification of 'Bharat Mata', the portrayal of the nation as a deity, continued unabated. Nobody really cared so much; it was left to the people to define how they wished to identify their nation. There was a rich historical backdrop of the freedom struggle but illiteracy, poverty and discriminations prevailing in the Indian society prevented the people from becoming well-versed with both their history and the laws laid down in the Constitution.

While the republic of India as established through the Constitution became the guiding light and symbolized the way of life people were meant to adopt and adhere to, jingoism differed in the sense that it hyped the reinvigoration of ancient India to proclaim a majoritarian view over the nation. Jingoists regard Muslims and Christians as foreign influences and demand the creation of a Hindu Rashtra for its majority population. That was precisely the reason why Gandhi was assassinated, and that's exactly what has led to the jingoistic environment that we now find ourselves in.

It may actually seem strange because 'Bharat Mata' is something we hear so often in India. This portrayal is older than Independence and was routinely used during the freedom movement too. It may also seem that we are invoking a goddess by hailing 'Bharat Mata', but what we often overlook is that it is the people who make the nation. Nehru addressed it in detail in *The Discovery of India* and we must revisit what he wrote:

> Sometimes as I reached a gathering, a great roar of welcome would greet me: Bharat Mata ki Jai—Victory to Mother India. I would ask them unexpectedly what they meant by that cry, who was this Bharat Mata, Mother India, whose victory they wanted? My question would amuse them and surprise them, and then, not knowing exactly what to answer, they would look at each other and at me. I persisted in my questioning. At last a vigorous Jat, wedded to the soil from immemorial generations, would say that it was the dharti, the good earth of India, that they meant. What earth? Their particular village patch, or all the patches in the district or province, or in the whole of India? And so question and answer went on, till they would ask me impatiently to tell them all about it. I would endeavour to do so and explain that India was all this that they had thought, but it was much more. The mountains and the rivers of India, and the forests and

the broad fields, which gave us food, were all dear to us, but what counted ultimately were the people of India…[57]

So, in a way, the people of India are themselves the solemn manifestation of Bharat Mata and they do not need to shout over each other to prove that their sense of belonging towards the nation is greater than their fellow countrymen. But by raising the tempo and speaking louder than everybody around them, jingoists lay seize over the vague idea of nationhood. Jingoism takes its shape by exploiting the vulnerabilities of the nation. It is, therefore, crucial to explore some of the issues of contention that are subject to exploitation in India:

1. Secularism:
One of the most striking features of independent India has been its ability to strive together despite its much diversity. After Independence, there was a conscious effort by Nehru to bridge the communal divide and bring the country together under one roof. But even before jingoism would acquire its current shape, politicians had already begun undermining secularism through vote banks and favours on religious grounds to remain in power. Things took an altogether different turn when riots broke out in 1984 against the Sikh community following Indira Gandhi's assassination. It came to be seen as a state-sponsored genocide, but the fiercest divisions have erupted between the Hindus and Muslims in the country time and again.

---

[57]"Who is Bharat Mata?" Jawaharlal Nehru's search for India,' *Reader's Digest*, 8 August 2019, https://www.readersdigest.in/conversations/story-the-search-for-india-124986, accessed 11 May 2021.

It is important to once again refer to the British policy of divide and rule, which was defeated with unity in diversity. India as a country comprises people of many religions and although secularism is sometimes seen as undermining religion, it actually stands to grant equal religious freedoms to all. It seeks to forbid discriminations on religious lines and becomes essential in ensuring that all citizens have dignity and pride of place in the patria.

People in India are generally aware of this. They quite know that instigations and provocations can lead to disturbances and, over the years, there have been several such instances when humanity has been shamed and hundreds of lives have been lost.

2. Pakistan:

India shares the strangest of relations with Pakistan. Formed after Partition in 1947, the two nations that were separated at birth have shared a rivalry ever since then. There have been numerous instances when peace initiatives have been launched but nothing has really yielded concrete results. The two countries have fought three wars, and the active participation of Indian troops tore Pakistan into two parts during the Bangladesh liberation war although it was likely to face the same fate sooner or later, given the disregard Pakistan showed towards its linguistic diversity.

India is routinely perturbed by terrorism that it says is harboured on Pakistani soil. Hundreds of Indians have lost their lives in terror attacks, bomb blasts and other gruesome acts of violence that have been apparently traced back to Pakistan. Several internationally designated terrorists spew venom against

India and pledge to bring mayhem to its soil while residing in comfort in Pakistan.

Tensions along the borders are routinely rife too. In such a complex scenario, Pakistan evokes mixed responses among most Indians. While not everybody supports military action or demands an all-out attack against our neighbour, there is no dearth of those who are sick and tired of waiting too. There are many who believe in improving the ties between the two nations and in promoting people-to-people connections, but then critics are of the opinion that these things cannot go hand in hand when ceasefire violations take place on a daily basis.

So, what does Pakistan really have to do with Indian patriotism? It becomes the defining ground when views, dissent or arguments are delegitimized by suggesting that they are sympathetic towards Pakistan. Jingoists exploit this vulnerability and use it as an excuse to hide their own errors or to justify their evil motives.

3. The Gandhi-Godse Debate:
There is no denying that Mahatma Gandhi is hailed as the Father of the Nation in India and that he is revered internationally too. But Gandhi was himself assassinated and even though independent India sought to value his teachings and legacy, the act of Godse, because it found its sense of purpose in the Hindu Rashtra, continues to be vigorously debated in India.

By and large, for most Indians even today, Gandhi is the tallest icon, but that does not change the fact that his life has been widely critiqued and evaluated. Therefore, it is important to understand the nuance of this debate. More than anything else, it becomes significant for us to remember Gandhi's assassination because that act was a betrayal of our freedom. The independence of India was not the end of the road as the nation freed from the clutches of imperialism had to be built from scratch. Gandhi was not only the champion of our freedom struggle but he also stood for a set of principles, of which satya and ahimsa were among the most significant. Now, it could very well be the case that everybody did not agree with Gandhi. Even a patriot could disagree with him, but the question in this case is how one disagreed. Gandhi spent his life urging Indians to shed violence and even led a nonviolent movement against the British, but he ultimately became its victim. Godse could disagree with Gandhi, debate with him or even challenge whatever Gandhi said. Instead, he chose to fire bullets and kill him.

This underlines the difference between the methods used by the two personalities. Gandhi did not want violence to become a tool to settle disputes and disagreements, but Godse did exactly that, which is why we must be conscious of this subtle difference.

4. Unity in Diversity:
It is something we hear very often in India. Politicians never cease to make mentions of it in their speeches while our history textbooks are also full of such references. It is very simple as it is a combination of two frequently used words. While 'unity' denotes the togetherness of people, 'diversity' implies the aspects that make them unique among each other. These range from religions and languages to practices and beliefs. Unity in diversity, thus, denotes the togetherness of the people

despite the things that make them unique.

In other words, from Tamils to Assamese and from Biharis to Gujaratis, all the people of India are tied together with the common thread of nationhood. This thread respects their diversity and gives them the freedom to practise their beliefs and customs. It holds that these are not barriers but rather bridges.

Jingoists, on the other hand, are hell-bent on proving their supremacy over others. If religion is a vexing factor, languages and eating habits also draw the ire of those who believe in the idea of 'Hindi-Hindu-Hindustan'. Therefore, tensions have often fuelled on linguistic lines too as India is a land of many languages and its people take pride in them. While they don't necessarily want to get rid of all those who have different ways of life, they surely also push for a unifying or a homogenous agenda that leads to confrontations.

For most of us, family is an integral part of our lives, it makes us feel safe but for Susannah, family was always a 'very dangerous place' to be in. It sometimes seemed like a 'nightmare of sorts' for her to grow up in that small Kerala village and all she wanted to do during those days was to escape. She says that she cannot really comprehend 'what exactly was so wrong' at her home that she left it and set out to live in a city she knew nothing about, had no means of livelihood and did not even know the language that people spoke in that part of the world. It was thus that Susannah Arundhati Roy left her home at 17.

In college too, she was known as Susannah to many of her friends, but Roy says that she 'just did not like Susannah' and so she 'got rid of it'. Perhaps, it was her own way of doing away with the memories of home that were associated with her family.

She struggled to make ends meet while she studied architecture in New Delhi. For several consecutive years after leaving home, the thoughts uppermost in her mind were how she would pay her rent or how she would last till the end of the month. She initially lived in the college hostel where she was studying architecture but soon ran short of money to pay the hostel and mess bills and had to move out to live in a slum near Feroz Shah Kotla. She lived through hell and used her memories and experiences to ease the pain. She fell in love, went to Goa and sold cakes on the beaches to make ends meet, broke her heart but fell in love again.[58] She was very whimsical by nature and could seem like a totally different person even for those who had known her. Ultimately, she didn't feel like inflicting herself on others because they didn't know what she would be tomorrow. She was onto something that occupied the entirety of her being. Maintaining that she had been a much-loved person, she sort of laments that by leaving people and moving away from them, she has inflicted pain.

'When you are loved so dearly and when you are this weird, you inflict pain upon others even if you don't necessarily want to. Sometimes I feel like a person with spikes, anywhere I turn somebody gets hurt,' she says.

She rose to prominence as the new deity of prose towards the end of the twentieth century and took the literary world by storm with the most astonishing, in a beautiful way, literary debut, *The God of Small Things*[59]. In October 1997, Roy became the first Indian writer to win the Booker Prize. Not only was

---

[58]Based on an interview with the author.
[59]Arundhati Boy, *The God of Small Things*, Penguin India; 1st edition, 2002.

it a shock in India but the reception that she garnered in the international press too showed how significant the moment was. 'The Booker for an Indian village love story? Till recently, such an outrageous suggestion would have been dismissed as a commendable piece of fiction. Now it is too true to be fiction,' *India Today* summarized this surprise in an article titled 'The New Deity of Prose' by Binoo K John.[60] Jason Cowley, one of the judges, said that *The God of Small Things* fulfilled the highest demand of fiction: to see the world, not conventionally or habitually, but as if for the first time.[61] Roy's achievement in the novel, according to Cowley, was never to forget about the small things in life: the insects and flowers, wind and water, the outcast and the despised.

As we progressed into the developing world order and as the reverberating boom of India…India…India…zipped through our ears and as rapid transformations were taking place all around us, the building wave of jingoism made success very complicated to deal with. And Roy experienced it first-hand.

'The impact of winning the Booker was tremendous. It happened so quickly that I had no time to absorb what was happening,' she recalls. The publication of *The God of Small*

---

[60]'Binoo K. John, 'Booker Prize winner Arundhati Roy brings recognition to Indo-Anglian writing,' *India Today*, 21 May 2013, https://www.indiatoday.in/magazine/cover-story/story/19971027-booker-prize-winner-arundhati-roy-brings-recognition-to-indo-anglian-writing-830808-1997-10-27, accessed 11 May 2021.

[61]'Booker prize judge Jason Cowley on why The God of Small Things was chosen,' *India Today*, 21 May 2013, https://www.indiatoday.in/magazine/cover-story/story/19971027-booker-prize-judge-jason-cowley-on-why-the-god-of-small-things-was-chosen-830818-1997-10-27, accessed 14 June 2021.

Things, her winning the Booker, and becoming a global figure and a literary celebrity in India, had all happened very quickly.

'It took a long time for me to deal with it afterwards because while it was a tremendous sense of accomplishment, at the same time, being the kind of person I am and living in a country where so many people can't read and don't have food, being successful in such an unfair and violent society is a bit complicated to deal with,' she says. Notwithstanding this complication, she emerged as a global phenomenon after winning the Booker Prize—an incredible voice of fiction from a third-world country, hailed gloriously at home too.

But then, in May 1998, India conducted its second nuclear test. Roy's famous line from *The God of Small Things*, 'Things can change in a day,' came back to haunt her. She criticized the nuclear test almost immediately. For many, it was as if she wanted to have a say in everything, that it was the narcissism of a fiction writer, her 'naïveté' to think that she could be taken seriously in matters of national security.[62] Was Roy unaware of the kind of response her staunch opposition to nuclear tests would bring in? What was the reason behind her sudden angst?

'What happened was that the timing of that test was so close to the time when I was being celebrated, that for me to stay quiet was as political as saying something. If I said nothing, somehow I was part of that celebration—a celebration that was repugnant to me,' she says.

Her world had died and she wrote *The End of Imagination*[63] to mourn its passing. And then, once again, things changed

---

[62]Based on personal interview with the author.
[63]Arundhati Roy, *The End of Imagination*, Haymarket Books, 2016.

in a day. Political and social Roy was born. The angst, lying dormant within her, found utterance after the bombs went off in India—and in Pakistan. 'That became the beginning of another kind of journey for me,' says Roy, who has since been at the forefront of many social, political and environmental struggles.

To understand why she was so angry, one needs to look at how she perceives nuclear weapons and what her views on it are. 'Nuclear weapons pervade our thinking. Control our behaviour. Administer our societies. Inform our dreams. They are the ultimate colonizer. Whiter than any white man that ever lived. The very heart of whiteness,' she wrote in *The End of Imagination*.[64]

But it was not limited to her reflections on the nuclear test alone. This time, unlike *The God of Small Things*, she was inciting the spirits of her readers through her carefully phrased sentences. She called on 'every man, woman and sentient child here in India, and over there, just a little way away in Pakistan', asking them to take these tests personally. 'The bomb isn't in your backyard. It's in your body. And mine. Nobody, no nation, no government, no man, no god, has the right to put it there. We're radioactive already, and the war hasn't even begun.'[65]

A nuclear-powered state, she says, is about all the philosophies behind the arrogance of man and that it should have the right to destroy the planet. 'Even without a war, the fact that you have nuclear weapons, to me, changed the acceptability of what can be said in public. That moment changed the public discourse in India, decisively,' she maintains.

---

[64]Ibid.
[65]Ibid.

She protested against what she called the implantation of a bomb in her brain, and if her resentment made her anti-Hindu or anti-national, she happily seceded, declaring herself 'an independent mobile republic'[66]. Roy had acquired the most solemn form of herself, a citizen of the earth who owned no flag or territory.[67] In the bruised national pride and the violent discourse of the time, warmongering became fashionable though it was frequently asserted that the nuclear weapons were to act as a deterrent. She reminded that if Lahore was bombed, Punjab too would burn, or Gujarat would be swallowed by flames if Karachi was bombed while Bombay and Rajasthan could also face the same fate. A nuclear war against Pakistan would not be a war against a foe but a war against ourselves.

As Roy took to activism, she was steadily removed from the world of fiction that had earned her global recognition. For her, there is a universe of difference between fiction and non-fiction. When she is writing non-fiction, she is writing usually with a tremendous sense of urgency. 'I am writing when something is closing down, some Supreme Court order has been issued or something very, very urgent requires intervention. And I am writing to intervene. I am writing to argue. I am writing to try and open a space for discourse,' she points out. Roy wrote critical essays and reported from the hinterlands on issues faced by the indigenous people. She felt that they had 'a far greater

[66]M.K. Raghavendra, 'The importance of being Arundhati Roy: As writer and political activist,' *FirstPost*, 18 June 2017, https://www.firstpost.com/living/the-importance-of-being-arundhati-roy-as-writer-and-political-activist-3708631.html, accessed 6 July 2021.
[67]Arundhati Roy, 'The End of Imagination (Bomb and I),' *The Algebra of Infinite Justice*, Penguin Books, 2013.

claim to being indigenous to this land than anybody else' and donated the Booker prize money for *The God of Small Things* to the Narmada Bachao Andolan. But it didn't really matter what her concerns were and nobody really bothered to think about the reasons why somebody who could have it all easy chose to speak up and change the course of her life. Her disdain for nuclear power, her relentless support to the cause of those she felt were being deliberately suppressed or preferably unheard was projected to suggest that she was an anti-Indian figure.[68] Her resentment was given a jingoistic fervour to suggest that she detested the nuclear test because of her sympathies for Pakistan[69] and ridiculous conspiracy theories began to float. But her open opposition to the nuclear test was only the prologue of the life she had set out to write for herself. Roy's position on Kashmir irked, and continues to severely irk a large section of people in India. She has, through her writings, maintained that India is an 'occupying force'[70] in Kashmir and has protested against the use of force and military in the Valley at national and international gatherings. Politicians, whether they were from the Bharatiya Janata Party (BJP) or the Congress, found solace in condemning her assertions and dismissing her fears by calling her a traitor.[71]

---

[68]Based on an interview with the author.

[69]Samanth Subramanian, 'The Prescient Anger of Arundhati Roy,' *The New Yorker*, 12 June 2019, https://www.newyorker.com/books/under-review/the-prescient-anger-of-arundhati-roy, accessed 14 June 2021.

[70]'What did Arundhati Roy say on Kashmir that prompted Paresh Rawal's obnoxious tweet?' *Daily O*, 25 May 2017, https://www.dailyo.in/variety/paresh-rawal-arundhati-roy-kashmir-sedition/story/1/17347.html, accessed 7 July 2021.

[71]Based on an interview with the author.

And then she did the unthinkable, said aloud what was meant to be brushed under the carpet. Expressing her utmost solidarity with the resistance movement in Kashmir, she alleged human rights violations and military occupation of the Valley by the Indian army.[72] That was unthinkable, how could she do something like that? Did she not know that Kashmir was as dear to Indians as to those she wanted the freedom for? That freedom had already come in 1947? That Jammu and Kashmir had acceded to India and not Pakistan? That the blood of Kashmiri Pandits had been shed, that they were forcefully thrown out of their homes, raped, murdered and butchered?

But then what do things like freedom mean to those whose collective memory is shaped by years of repression? She pointed to the tens of thousands of Kashmiris who had been killed, who had simply disappeared, who were tortured, injured, raped and humiliated, and sought justice for them.[73] She argued that when their rage finds utterance, it could not be 'tamed, rebottled and sent back to where it came from'[74]. Roy has also drawn criticism for condemning the state of affairs in India with hype and euphoria in her speeches abroad. If her prose spells magic, her assertions create panic.

We must leave this tracing of Roy's forays in the Valley for some time, if only to return to the building wave of jingoism

---

[72]Arundhati Roy, 'The dead begin to speak up in India,' *The Guardian*, 30 September 2011, https://www.theguardian.com/commentisfree/libertycentral/2011/sep/30/kashmir-india-unmarked-graves, accessed 18 May 2021.
[73]Covered in an interview with the author.
[74]Arundhati Roy, 'Land and Freedom,' *The Guardian*, 22 August 2008, https://www.theguardian.com/world/2008/aug/22/kashmir.india, accessed 12 July 2021.

in India and how its currents gradually obliterated the existence of criticism, of contrarian view, of argument, of the ability to have empathy, and above all, of the very nature of freedom in a free nation.

In the late 1970s, several members in the Morarji Desai government had sought changes in history textbooks. The books that were being targeted by the Jan Sangh members included two significant works by Romila Thapar, *Medieval India* written by her and *Communalism and the Writing of Indian History*, which she wrote along with Harbans Mukhia and Bipan Chandra. Those protesting against these books criticized Thapar for several reasons, primarily for going soft on some Muslim rulers.[75]

'I did not allow the textbooks written by me to be changed because every time they would want to make a change, I would say "yes, go ahead and make a change, just take my name off the book". But they didn't want to do that because they wanted the legitimacy of the name of a historian and yet they wanted to make the changes,' she recalls.[76]

More trouble was brewing for Thapar when she was removed from the Indian Council of Historical Research in less than three months after the BJP came to power in 1999.[77]

There was silence for some time but after merely four years, the vitriol reached its peak once again in 2003 when she was appointed as the Visiting Chair at the Library of Congress. She was supposed to spend 10 months at the John W. Kluge Center

---

[75]Based on an interview with the author.
[76]Ibid.
[77]Praveen Swami, 'Ideas of history,' *The Hindu*, 21 May 2016, https://www.thehindu.com/features/magazine/ideas-of-history/article5875979.ece, accessed 7 July 2021.

pursuing 'Historical Consciousness in Early India' as her area of research, but a petition against her appointment described her as a 'Marxist' and 'anti-Hindu', while emphasizing that it was 'a waste of US money to support a Leftist'.[78]

'Within a month of my reaching Washington, there was a 15-page-long petition saying the most vicious things about me. Really, I mean written by people after reading whom one could make out how paranoid they were. I was terribly disturbed at that point of time. I wondered what to do next. Here I was, sitting in Washington, alone. I knew nobody in the embassy, I knew nobody in the Library of Congress. I wondered how I was going to manage this attack,' she recalls.

Finally, she was assured by responsible people at the Library of Congress that they were not going to make any changes as far as the protest was concerned. Prof. Thapar was told that they had evaluated her work before the appointment and as a result they were not going to be perturbed by the protests against her. Now that she was relieved, she faced the question of whether to respond or not.

'Do I respond? Or do I just keep quiet? The problem with responding was that one would then have to respond each time somebody wrote against one. A couple of senior academics in London (ex-teachers of mine and so on) wrote to me and said that for God's sake don't respond because that's exactly what they want you to do. They will want you to spend all your

---

[78]Covered in interviews; additionally Romila Thapar, Ramin Jahanbegloo and Neeladri Bhattacharya, *Talking History: Romila Thapar in conversation with Ramin Jahanbegloo, with the participation of Neeladri Bhattacharya*, 1st Edition. Oxford University Press, 2017.

time defending yourself on stupid issues whereas you should be doing serious research. And so I thought about it at great length and eventually I decided not to respond and I haven't for that reason, although they all call me a coward, they say I am not willing to have a public debate and so on. And my attitude is that as an academic, I am not into public debate, I write what I think is right, I give my evidence, I give my references. Take it or leave it. I am not insisting that you should follow what I say,' she maintains.[79]

While she may be revered and respected globally as a master historian, jingoists are opposed to her views and they make their disagreement with her public quite frequently.

'I think the main point is the insistence that I have the right to research and write and give evidence for what I am saying and make my statement about the past. I think this is the right that everybody has and why should I be denied that right which everybody has?' she asks.

She maintains that arguing a particular position in any discipline is a constitutional mandate as long as she sticks to the given methodology and substantiates her research with enough evidence. This is also where she makes a distinction between 'academic history' and 'fantasy history'. Fantasy history, she says, is written for public consumption. 'But I have been firm on the fact that as an academic historian, I will go on saying what I wish to say, on the basis of my research.'

She says that in all political movements, history plays a crucial role. 'These movements get their legitimacy from history. They justify themselves from history, so for them, it's terribly

---

[79]Based on an interview with the author.

important that their history gets accepted and not ours. And that we are challenging their history is something they consider dangerous for them. So, it's not even at the level of historical writing and historical explanation, it's also a political battle, which is what makes it so vicious,' she adds.

What we are often made to forget is that the sense of belonging is very natural and most people find comfort in it, but that does not mean it becomes the centre of their existence. People go about their lives and they do the things they do, they have a say in the society and participate in national affairs. Therefore, even if one disagrees with you or does not necessarily share the same views as you, one does not become unpatriotic. Patriotism is about the people. The contestation against secular and democratic values of India by jingoists is largely on the grounds that India should become a Hindu Rashtra because of its historical roots. But a historian who flipped back the pages of history and came up with her research works that questioned such legitimacy became a target of unprecedented vitriol. That's the nature of jingoism that crushes dissent and rational thinking in the name of blind patriotism.

During this turbulent phase when India was racing against time, Shashi had resigned as United Nations (UN) under secretary-general for public information after contesting for the secretary-generalship at the UN. But he soon found himself to be pining to do something real and participate in nation-building. He was approached by the BJP, the Congress and the Left to plunge into politics,[80] but he ultimately

---

[80]'BJP, Left among others wanted me to join them: Congress MP Shashi Tharoor,' *The Economic Times*, 12 December 2015, https://economictimes.

joined the Congress in 2009. He says his inclinations and understanding of India naturally seem to meet with India's grand old party. He was rising through the ranks just as his reach was multiplying among Indians caught in the frenzy of the internet revolution.

Distortion of history and misinformation had become everyday phenomena. Ghosts from the pages of history were resurrected even as a conscious attempt of polarization was made by suggesting that the majority population in India had never gotten their due and that a 'Hindu Hriday Samrat' (King of Hindus' heart) would transform their lives.

The rise of social media and the rapid spread of smartphones in India redefined its society like never before. For most millennials in India, the internet arrived at a very slow pace. They were first introduced to computers in their schools, where they were probably required to open their shoes outside the computer laboratories. Then came the cyber cafes. The internet became available at homes much later. But the coming of smartphones narrowed the gaps. Information, which was so far a privilege and not within everybody's reach, suddenly became very easily accessible. And people found all sorts of things coming directly into their instant messaging applications. What seemed simply unacceptable till yesterday became forwards that were widely circulated among Indians, particularly those residing in the Hindi heartland. These included vicious and divisive messages, and politically motivated and fake news.

indiatimes.com/news/politics-and-nation/bjp-left-among-others-wanted-me-to-join-them-congress-mp-shashi-tharoor/articleshow/50152262.cms, accessed 14 June 2021.

It is important to note that this was also the time when there was a fuming anger against the ruling Congress party. Corruption and inequality in India had risen while people were still starving and dying of hunger. It had been almost seven decades since Independence, but India was still lagging behind, its people were still poor and its farmers were still killing themselves. The anger of the people was instigated by the Anna Hazare Movement of 2011 when a series of demonstrations and protests rocked India. They were intended to establish strong legislation and enforcement against political corruption and set the stage for an all-out battle in the 2014 Lok Sabha elections, which ultimately resulted in the victory of Narendra Modi-led BJP. The party that Shashi represented in the Indian parliament had long lost its original character that was instrumental in India's struggle for freedom. Much of the power to dictate the party affairs was confined in the hands of the Nehru-Gandhi family even after the Emergency. It seemed as if every other leader within the party, regardless of their talent, dedication, commitment or struggles, were secondary.[81]

The BJP has had a communal agenda at its core and it has never been shy of saying it out loud,[82] but Modi sought to present himself as an inclusive leader who promised to work for 'sabka saath, sabka vikas, sabka vishwas' (Together, for everyone's growth, with everyone's trust). He took below-the-

---

[81]Sadanand Dhume, 'The House of Nehru-Gandhi,' *Foreign Policy*, 20 July 2012, https://foreignpolicy.com/2012/07/20/the-house-of-nehru-gandhi/, accessed 14 June 2021.

[82]'How the BJP promotes Hindutva through a Nationalist Agenda,' EPW Engage, 6 May 2019, https://www.epw.in/engage/article/how-bjp-promotes-hindutva-through-nationalist, accessed 14 June 2021.

belt jibes at the 'shahzada' (prince), the scion of the Nehru-Gandhi family,[83] which he blamed for ruling the country for all the years after Independence. Such banters among politicians are nothing new and all sides use them in their rallies and campaigns. The most outstanding feature of Modi's rise was the promises he made. Young Indians were swayed by his hyperboles just while they were learning the new habit of spending hours on the smartphone. He promised to transform the country's economy, create new jobs for the young population, build better universities and save the farmers from their misery.

Even some of the most vehement of Modi's critics argued that there was a ray of hope in his rise. The anguished majority population of India, the Hindus to be more precise, had felt a sense of betrayal by the successive Congress regime. The over-the-top attempts of the State to portray India as a secular State, many felt, had resulted in a gradual but steady obliteration of Hindu festivities and celebrations. The Congress party had so far controlled the mechanisms by which information was shared with the public. It had a monopoly over public discourse,[84] but things changed with the rise of social media and resulted in a transformation in public perception.

---

[83]Akash Deep Ashok, 'Modi's barbs at "Shahzada" and "Madam": No-holds-barred political rhetoric of 2013,' *India Today*, 7 November 2013, https://www.indiatoday.in/india/story/narendra-modi-sonia-gandhi-rahul-gandhi-congress-bjp-shahzada-216761-2013-11-07, accessed 14 June 2021.
[84]Minhaz Merchant, 'Why India no longer trusts anti-Modi media,' Daily O, 27 November 2017, https://www.dailyo.in/politics/modi-government-indian-media-hindu-taliban-sonia-gandhi-congress-bjp-upa/story/1/7638.html, accessed 14 June 2021.

7

The Great Betrayal

What began as hope turned into desperation. This was followed by the breakdown of social security nets as the government of the day indulged in open divisive politics and gradually took the shape of despair that India currently finds itself engulfed in. Modi's rise as the prime minister of India could be attributed to several factors, but the most prominent among them were his promises to curb corruption[85] which had gained prominence during the Congress-led United Progressive Alliance (UPA)-II government, to create jobs and uplift the Indian economy as he used a slew of rhetoric and hyperboles[86] that catered to the aspiring population

---

[85]'UPA report card: Nine years, nine scams,' *India Today*, https://www.indiatoday.in/india/photo/upa-govt-9-years-9-scams-sonia-manmohan-369868-2013-05-22, accessed 12 May 2021.
[86]Sneha Alexander, 'As election campaign intensifies so does hyperbole from both sides,' *Mint*, 13 May 2019, https://www.livemint.com/elections/lok-

of India. At the same time, he was backed by a battery of social media influencers, who portrayed him as the only alternative at that crucial juncture when protests against the gruesome rape of Nirbhaya and the anti-corruption movement led by Anna Hazare and Arvind Kejriwal had multiplied the participation of the general public in the national discourse by manifold.[87]

The television news channels were swayed by Modi's popularity just as advertisements with catchy slogans such as '*Abki baar, Modi sarkar* (This time, it's gonna be Modi government)' flooded the streets and loudspeakers announcing the development he brought in Gujarat made heavy inroads in rural India. Backed by the foot soldiers of the Rashtriya Swayamsevak Sangh (RSS), its affiliates and other far-right groups, the door-to-door campaigns that catapulted Modi to the top post were something that Indian elections had never seen before.

Modi's official website (www.narendramodi.in) itself makes a note of the scale of his election campaign, and stresses that such an election campaign had never been undertaken in India previously.

When the history of this election will be written, one thing that will stand out is the historic campaign undertaken by Narendra Modi to reach out to the people of India in

sabha-elections/as-election-campaign-intensifies-so-does-hyperbole-from-both-sides-1557733607648.html, accessed 14 June 2021.
[87]Anuja and Pretika Khanna, 'Anti-corruption movement a watershed moment in India,' *Mint*, 13 December 2019, https://www.livemint.com/news/india/anti-corruption-movement-a-watershed-moment-in-india-11576199569995.html, accessed 16 June 2021.

order to convey the message of development and good governance. Never before in India's electoral history has a leader emerged as such a bright ray of hope for people. Never before has a campaign been undertaken with so much innovation and precision. It would not be an exaggeration to describe the Modi campaign as one of the biggest mass mobilisation exercise seen anywhere in the history of electioneering. The scale and intensity of the campaign becomes even bigger when one understands the large population and geographic spread of India. Yes, in the past, political leaders have led marathon campaigns but the scale at which this campaign has been done beats them all by miles![88]

Between 15 September 2013 and 10 May 2014, the would-be prime minister addressed nearly 5,827 rallies, programmes and events. He covered a total distance of over 3 lakh km, visited each of the states of India, presenting a unique vision for each state and used unprecedented innovation as seen during 3D rallies and Chai Pe Charcha.

A proud nationalist, who had risen from very humble beginnings, Modi made patriotism the epicentre of his election campaign. He skilfully showed one side of the picture to the voters, castigating the Congress and the Nehru-Gandhi family for the sordid state of India's poor. He hyped the strength of the Indian armed forces and made repeated references to their valour. To Modi, there was a war to be won and not just a national election. In fact, in his first speech after being

---

[88]Narendra Modi, https://www.narendramodi.in/largest-mass-outreach-campaign-in-electoral-history-of-a-democracy-3136, accessed 12 May 2021.

declared the BJP's prime ministerial candidate, Modi referred to patriotism and the Indian army to suit his electoral needs. He was speaking at a rally in Haryana's Rewari on 15 September 2013. He raged against being selective on the issue of terror, impressed upon the valour and sacrifice of the armed forces and said that one cannot imagine the amount of courage that is there in this land.[89] He incited the spirit of his countrymen living in far-flung villages and rural hamlets by suggesting that the then government was somehow partnering with Pakistan to damage the strength and morale of the Indian army. And just when one looked at him from the other side, it seemed like a shameful thing to do—to suggest that the government ruling India was not working for India, but he used his oratory skills to attract the voters.[90] It was tempting to find hope in the man who has ruled the roost in India ever since then. How I wish that the things he said back then did not vanish from his agenda soon after he assumed office.

The power of hyperboles and rhetoric that were multiplied by the rise of social media have curbed our ability to see through things with sanity and rational thinking.

It was, therefore, that his lucratively funded election[91]

[89]'Nation is very proud of our servicemen, who make sacrifices for the nation: Narendra Modi at Rewari,'15 September 2013, https://www.narendramodi. in/nation-is-very-proud-of-our-servicemen-who-make-sacrifices-for-the-nation-narendra-modi-at-rewari-5545, accessed 12 May 2021.
[90]Ibid.
[91]Devjyot Ghoshal and Manu Balachandran, 'It cost Narendra Modi $100 million to win the Indian election—here's how he spent it,' QUARTZ INDIA, 16 January 2015, https://qz.com/india/327771/it-cost-narendra-modi-100-million-to-win-the-indian-election-heres-how-he-spent-it/, accessed 14 June 2021.

campaign made it seem to the general public that good days are coming (*acche din aane wale hain*). His predecessor, Dr Manmohan Singh, a soft-spoken and fine gentleman, had warned his countrymen that Modi as the prime minister would be a disaster for India,[92] but his opponent used his fine oratory skills to delegitimize Dr Singh's proclamations by stating that his government was being run through a remote control by the Nehru-Gandhi family[93].

Despite the heated political environment, Modi's rise stood to symbolize the strength and tenacity of Indian democracy, where an absolute nobody would rise from his battered childhood to become the challenger for the country's premiership. That his opponent was the scion of the Nehru-Gandhi dynasty became his most powerful weapon. As he waxed eloquent about his struggles as a chaiwallah,[94] the Indian public found a strange solace in giving an opportunity to a commoner as him as opposed to the grandson of Mrs Gandhi, who had declared the Emergency. Modi's campaign had skilfully maligned the image of the Nehru-Gandhi family, holding it responsible for

[92]ANI, '"It will be a disaster if Modi becomes PM of India," says Manmohan Singh,' *Business Standard*, 3 January 2014, https://www.business-standard.com/article/news-ani/it-will-be-a-disaster-if-modi-becomes-pm-of-india-says-manmohan-singh-11401030,0297_1.html, accessed 12 May 2021.

[93]PTI, 'UPA government "remote controlled": Narendra Modi,' *The Economic Times*, 13 April 2014, https://economictimes.indiatimes.com/news/politics-and-nation/upa-government-remote-controlled-narendra-modi/articleshow/33700351.cms?from=mdr, accessed 12 May 2021.

[94]Ayeshea Perara, 'Modi Live: "India will support the chaiwallah on the battlefield",' *Firstpost*, 19 January 2014, https://www.firstpost.com/politics/modi-live-india-will-support-the-chaiwallah-on-the-battlefield-1347623.html, accessed 14 June 2021.

all the ills that plagued India while cunningly stealing the credit for all things good.

As he rode to power, Mr Prime Minister denied the assertions of his liberal critics, contested that he would be a divisive figure by claiming that his government had a responsibility to take everyone with them.[95] Working as a journalist, watching Modi's rise to the Centre and seeing things unfold in the manner that they did, one could gauge the upheaval that was awaiting India quite early during his days as the prime minister. There began to emerge clear contradictions between what the all-powerful man said and did, or allowed to be done in the name of Bharat Mata.[96] Modi was something different, made of 'sterner stuff', he was no Nehru to explain to the public that Bharat Mata was the manifestation of the people of India. Instead, Mr Prime Minister used it to embolden a monolithic image of India. Bharat Mata became a mythological figure as we watched our country plunge into unimaginable intolerance, hate and bigotry.[97] All of this happened so quickly that our beloved India began to stink and suffocate its inmates with unprecedented vitriol that became a matter of everyday news cycle.

[95]Oliver Laughland and Matthew Weaver, 'Indian election result: 2014 is Modi's year as BJP secures victory,' *The Guardian*, 16 May 2014, https://www.theguardian.com/world/2014/may/16/india-election-2014-results-live, accessed 12 May 2021.
[96]ANI, 'Narendra Modi a paradoxical Prime Minister: Dr Manmohan Singh,' *Business Standard*, 27 October 2018, https://www.business-standard.com/article/news-ani/narendra-modi-a-paradoxical-prime-minister-dr-manmohan-singh-118102700046_1.html, accessed 14 June 2021.
[97]Anindita Sanyal, 'PM Modi's Jibe at Manmohan Singh over "Bharat Mata Ki Jai",' NDTV, 3 March 2020, https://www.ndtv.com/india-news/pm-narendra-modi-jibe-at-manmohan-singh-over-bharat-mata-ki-jai-2188945, accessed 14 June 2021.

Things took a sinister shape with the deliberate politics of love jihad, *ghar wapsi* (back to home) and cow vigilantes.[98] Reports of minorities, particularly Muslims and Dalits, being thrashed by far-right mobs, and abated by cops at many instances[99] became so rife that writing and reporting about them became an exercise of immense psychological trauma. We were all being lured into an echo chamber from which there was no escaping. It was as if everything we had been proud of about our nation was fading into oblivion; things that we had taken for granted, never really cared or bothered about, were being deliberately throttled and pushed into a massive black hole while a new India was being forcefully thrust upon us. Those who resisted it did so at their own peril. From journalists being issued rape and death threats to career historians being subjugated and deprived of their hard-earned positions, the dissenting voices in India were faced with numerous challenges.

Mr Prime Minister's social media units had so catastrophically manipulated the understanding of nationhood that criticizing the government, or even mildly opposing its

---

[98]'BJP's "Love Jehad" Politics: Hating Love, Loving Hate,' CPIML, https://www.cpiml.net/liberation/2021/01/bjps-love-jehad-politics-hating-love-loving-hate, accessed 14 June 2021; PTI, '2014 saw controversies over "love-jihad", "ghar-wapsi",' *The Economic Times*, 30 December 2014, https://economictimes.indiatimes.com/news/politics-and-nation/2014-saw-controversies-over-love-jihad-ghar-wapsi/articleshow/45685267.cms, accessed 14 June 2021.

[99]'After Madhya Pradesh, Muslim man thrashed in Gurugram; "told to remove skullcap and chant Bharat Mata Ki Jai",' Times Now, 26 May 2019, https://www.timesnownews.com/india/article/after-madhya-pradesh-muslim-man-thrashed-in-gurugram-told-to-remove-skullcap-and-chant-bharat-mata-ki-jai/425646, accessed 14 June 2021.

policies and suggesting anything that differed from its line of thought began to be seen as a criminal exercise.[100]

My country began to bleed but it was only the beginning of the brutal desecration of India's inclusive character. Strange murmurs ran through newsrooms every evening as reporters returned from their respective fields with horrific stories. From hospitals to schools and colleges, there was an upsurge in agony among the masses, but the heavy-handedness of the government and law-enforcing agencies had forced the public to become mute spectators. It was just yesterday that the singing of the national anthem evoked a sense of national pride and unity; it wasn't something that we forced upon one another, but the upbringing of most Indians had regarded national unity and integration as part and parcel of our lives. But here we were, facing the strange turn of events when emboldened mobs were deliberately forcing people to sing the national anthem and chant '*Bharat Mata ki Jai*'.[101] This was being carried out without the slightest realization that every Indian was equal in the eyes of the law and that

---

[100]Cyril Sam and Paranjoy Guha Thakurta, 'Meet the advisors who helped make the BJP a social media powerhouse of data and propaganda,' *Scroll.in*, 6 May 2019, https://scroll.in/article/922371/meet-the-advisors-who-helped-make-the-bjp-a-social-media-powerhouse-of-data-and-propaganda, accessed 14 June 2021; Regina Mihindukulasuriya, 'Nearly 18,000 Twitter accounts spread "fake news" for BJP, 147 do it for Congress: Study,' *The Print*, 31 January 2020, https://theprint.in/politics/nearly-18000-twitter-accounts-spread-fake-news-for-bjp-147-do-it-for-congress-study/356876/, accessed 14 June 2021.
[101]Outlook Web Bureau, 'Muslim man dragged out of mosque, forced to say "Bharat Mata ki Jai" allegedly by Bajrang Dal activists In Hisar,' *Outlook*, 13 July 2017, https://www.outlookindia.com/website/story/muslim-man-dragged-out-of-mosque-forced-to-say-bharat-mata-ki-jai-by-bajrang-dal/299556, accessed 18 May 2021.

the national anthem was the unique identity of every Indian. It wasn't something that one could force upon another, but the government did not do enough and often became the most powerful enabler of such horrific acts.[102] With every passing day, prominent issues such as healthcare, economy, agriculture and jobs were sidelined, whereas a communal and divisive agenda became the modus operandi of the regime.[103] It was all in the open, things were being done in broad daylight, and yet, there was so little shame. What was really baffling at that point in time was the fact that the British policy of divide and rule had been reinstated in India with double vigour. Illiteracy of the people was used as a tool to weaponize the communal agenda through rapid spread of fake news and misinformation.[104] While all of this was happening in India, under the prime ministership of Modi, public intellectuals, writers, artistes and historians could decipher a sinister plan for which pillars were being laid and old institutions were being crumbled to dust.

While there were numerous reports of minorities being marginalized in many parts of India, there were also cases that shook the nerves of those who were resisting the changing face of India. Among these, the murders of author and Maharashtrian

---

[102]Paulomi Saha, 'Some find foul smell in saying Bharat Mata Ki Jai: PM Modi hits out at Manmohan Singh,' *India Today*, 3 March 2020, https://www.indiatoday.in/india/story/pm-narendra-modi-manmohan-singh-bharat-mata-ki-jai-slogan-row-1651856-2020-03-03, accessed 14 June 2021.
[103]Pooja Chaudhuri, 'Amit Malviya's fake news fountain: 16 pieces of misinformation spread by the BJP IT cell chief,' *Scroll.in*, 10 February 2021, https://scroll.in/article/952731/amit-malviyas-fake-news-fountain-16-pieces-of-misinformation-spread-by-the-bjp-it-cell-chief, accessed 14 June 2021.
[104]Ibid.

libertarian Narendra Dabholkar, author and politician Govind Pansare and Karnataka philosopher M.M. Kalburgi were the most troubling. These were rational thinkers who challenged superstitious practices, but even while they were killed, members of the dispensation failed to take note of it and instead maintained a strange silence as if nothing had happened. At that stage, silence became a betrayal even though speaking up meant putting one at similar risks.

Just as these things were unfolding one after the other, the India that Mahatma Gandhi fought to free was being laid to rest as Muslims began to be sidelined and targeted. The lynching of Mohammed Akhlaq in Uttar Pradesh's Dadri on the suspicion of cow slaughter was the beginning of a dreadful chapter in independent India that was sought to be written with the cold blood of Muslims.[105] It was outrightly ignored that the independence of India promised equality to all its citizens and it was made binding upon the state to foster brotherhood among its population. Indians were Indians in their life as citizens of the country, they were not Muslims or Hindus or Christians or Parsis. Our patriotism meant respecting our diversity and strengthening our unity but under Modi's rule, the atmosphere became so vitiated that the quest for a Hindu Rashtra gained ground once again.[106] The debates that had been settled in 1950 with the adoption of the Constitution of India remained out of sight and out of mind of the frenzied mobs who were dead-

---

[105]'Indian man lynched over beef rumours,' BBC News, 30 September 2015, https://www.bbc.com/news/world-asia-india-34398433, accessed 12 May 2021.
[106]Ramesh Thakur, 'Modi's project to make a Hindu India,' *The Japan Times*, 13 January 2020, https://www.japantimes.co.jp/opinion/2020/01/13/commentary/world-commentary/modis-project-make-hindu-india/, accessed 14 June 2021.

drunk in the cocktail of religious fanaticism and propaganda harboured through WhatsApp.

Such events, even while they were ignored by the government, resulted in public anger against the building wave of intolerance in a country that was once known for its brotherhood and harmony. Till yesterday, India had been a shining example of communal harmony to the world. Countries across the globe looked up to this nation of great diversity and sought to instill the values that had helped write the glorious tale of India. As things evolved and more blood dripped, fears began to mount. Speaking up against a regime that enjoyed a brute majority and was drunk with arrogance became an uphill task.

Writers and artists sounded the bugle. Perturbed by the silence of the Sahitya Akademi, India's National Academy of Letters, on the killing of the three rational thinkers, including an Akademi awardee, scores of recipients of the prestigious award began to return their awards in protest against growing intolerance and hatred in India.[107] Writers from all over the country accused the Sahitya Akademi of having failed to perform its duty as the custodian of literary freedom and raised questions over the autonomy of the body in the light of its failure to speak up against the establishment.[108] As a journalist covering

---

[107]*India Today* Web Desk, 'More than 25 writers return their Sahitya Akademi Awards in protest,' *India Today*, 16 October 2015, https://www.indiatoday.in/education-today/gk-current-affairs/story/sahitya-akademi-award-268296-2015-10-15, accessed 14 June 2021.

[108]Ashutosh Bharadwaj, 'The Sahitya Akademi row: All you need to know,' *The Indian Express*, 14 October 2015, https://indianexpress.com/article/explained/writers-protest-what-returning-sahitya-akademi-honour-means/, accessed 12 May 2021.

these protests first-hand in September 2015, one saw the angst of those who normally spend their time in solitude. Elderly writers marched to Rabindra Bhavan in the national capital and demanded that the Akademi made it absolutely clear to the government that it will not remain a mute spectator to the assaults against creative freedom.[109]

It was a powerful statement but a heart-breaking sight. The finest voices of the country were out on the streets against the hatred that was building in India, but the arrogant regime was simply unwilling to listen to them.[110] The movement that came to be known as the Award Wapsi protest reached its crescendo when Nayantara Sahgal returned the prestigious honour. An eminent Indian author and niece of the country's first prime minister, Nehru, Sahgal returned the Sahitya Akademi award in protest against increasing intolerance towards right to dissent in the country and Modi's 'silence' on the 'reign of terror'.[111]

'The ruling ideology today is a fascist ideology and that is what is worrying me now. We did not have a fascist government until now... I am doing whatever I believe in,' she said in an interview.[112] Citing various incidents of killings of writers

---

[109]Nayantara Sahgal, 'The unmaking of India: Why writer Nayantara Sahgal is returning her Sahitya Akademi Award,' *Scroll.in*, 6 October 2015, https://scroll.in/article/760247/the-unmaking-of-india-why-writer-nayantara-sahgal-is-returning-her-sahitya-akademi-award, accessed 14 June 2021.
[110]Seema Chisthi, 'Writers protest: government should respect The Word,' *The Indian Express*, 13 October 2015, https://indianexpress.com/article/explained/writers-protest-government-should-respect-the-word/, accessed 14 June 2021.
[111]PTI, 'Nayantara Sahgal returns Sahitya Akademi award to protest rising intolerance,' *Mint*, 6 October 2015, https://www.livemint.com/Politics/zONZfHUAfEn1Ix0JhQAhNP/Nayantara-returns-Sahitya-Akademi-Award-protests-rising-int.html, accessed 12 May 2021.
[112]Ibid.

and rationalists, including Kalburgi and Pansare, she alleged, 'Rationalists who question superstition, anyone who questions any aspect of the ugly and dangerous distortion of Hinduism known as Hindutva—whether in the intellectual or artistic sphere, or whether in terms of food habits and lifestyle—are being marginalised, persecuted, or murdered,' she spoke out in disgust.[113]

Sahgal referred to the most recent incident of a village blacksmith, Mohammed Akhlaq, who was dragged out of his home and brutally lynched on mere suspicion that beef was cooked in his home. She further added:

> In all these cases, justice drags its feet. The Prime Minister remains silent about this reign of terror. We must assume he dare not alienate evil-doers who support his ideology. It is a matter of sorrow that the Sahitya Akademi remains silent… In memory of the Indians who have been murdered, in support of all Indians who uphold the right to dissent, and of all dissenters who now live in fear and uncertainty, I am returning my Sahitya Akademi Award.[114]

Sahgal said that Modi was a politician who knew how to speak. She recalled that he had given long speeches and was vocal on Twitter and other social media platforms too and demanded that

---

[113]'Writer returns award to protest Modi "silence on intolerance",' BBC, 7 October 2015, https://www.bbc.com/news/world-asia-india-34461911, accessed 14 June 2021.
[114]PTI, 'Nayantara Sahgal returns Sahitya Akademi award to protest rising intolerance,' *Mint*, 6 October 2015, https://www.livemint.com/Politics/zONZfHUAfEn1Ix0JhQAhNP/Nayantara-returns-Sahitya-Akademi-Awardprotests-rising-int.html, accessed 12 May 2021..

he should be responsible for what was happening in the country.[115]

She went on to add that under Modi's government, India was going backwards, it was rejecting its great idea of cultural diversity and debate and it was narrowing down to an invention called Hindutva.[116] The writer in her open letter, 'The Unmaking of India', said it was 'a matter of sorrow' that the Sahitya Akademi was silent on these issues.[117] 'In protest against Kalburgi's murder, a Hindi writer, Uday Prakash, has returned his Sahitya Akademi Award. Six Kannada writers have returned their awards to the Kannada Sahitya Parishat,' she said. She stated that the right to dissent was an integral part of the constitutional guarantee.[118]

What was a scathing statement by one of India's most respected authors came across as an opportunity to the dispensation to discredit and demonize the entire movement.[119] The supporters of the government jumped at her immediately, alleging that she was doing nothing but carrying out the agenda of the Congress party, that she was helping the Nehru-Gandhi family, to which she belonged, to harm the reputation of India

---

[115]Ibid.

[116]Ibid.

[117]Nayantara Sahgal, 'The unmaking of India: Why writer Nayantara Sahgal is returning her Sahitya Akademi Award,' *Scroll.in*, 6 October 2015, https://scroll.in/article/760247/the-unmaking-of-india-why-writer-nayantara-sahgal-is-returning-her-sahitya-akademi-award, accessed 12 May 2021.

[118]Ibid.

[119]'Writer Nayantara Sahgal returns her Sahitya Akademi Award,' News 18, 6 October 2015, https://www.news18.com/news/india/writer-nayantara-sahgal-returns-her-sahitya-akademi-award-in-protest-against-governments-failure-to-safeguard-cultural-diversity-1144900.html, accessed 12 May 2021.

in the international eye.[120] In doing so, it was completely ignored that Sahgal had, in the past, also strongly criticized the imposition of the Emergency in 1975 by her cousin, late prime minister Indira Gandhi.

The unprecedented movement during the very early days of the Modi government was joined by dozens of scientists, filmmakers and artists too.[121] While an atmosphere of fear and bigotry was just beginning to cast its shadows over India, Arundhati Roy, though full well aware of the castigation that was going to follow, lent her support to the cause.[122] She issued the following statement.

Today, we live in a country in which, when the thugs and apparatchiks of the New Order talk of 'illegal slaughter', they mean the imaginary cow that was killed—not the real man who was murdered. When they talk of taking 'evidence for forensic examination' from the scene of the crime, they mean the food in the fridge, not the body of the lynched man. We say we have 'progressed', but when Dalits are

---

[120]'Award wapsi to defame India: Anupam Kher leads march against intolerance protests,' *Firstpost*, 7 November 2015, https://www.firstpost.com/india/award-wapsi-to-defame-india-anupam-kher-leads-march-against-intolerance-protests-2498828.html, accessed 14 June 2021.

[121]Humaira Ansar and Kanika Sharma, 'And it continues: 24 more filmmakers, writers return awards,' *Hindustan Times*, 26 November 2015, https://www.hindustantimes.com/india/and-it-continues-kundan-shah-saeed-mirza-join-award-wapsi/story-t7guKRzkGv7ZrsTY6vOMZJ.html, accessed 14 June 2021.

[122]Hannah Ellis-Petersen, 'Arundhati Roy returns award in protest against religious intolerance in India,' *The Guardian*, 5 November 2015, https://www.theguardian.com/books/2015/nov/05/arundhati-roy-returns-award-protest-religious-intolerance-india-bollywood-modi-government-violence, accessed 12 May 2021.

butchered and their children burned alive, which writer today can freely say, like Babasaheb Ambedkar once did, that 'to the untouchables, Hinduism is a veritable chamber of horrors', without getting attacked, lynched, shot or jailed? Which writer can write what Saadat Hasan Manto wrote in his 'Letters to Uncle Sam'? It doesn't matter whether we agree or disagree with what is being said. If we do not have the right to speak freely, we will turn into a society that suffers from intellectual malnutrition, a nation of fools. Across the subcontinent it has become a race to the bottom—one that the New India has enthusiastically joined. Here too now, censorship has been outsourced to the mob.

I am very pleased to have found (from somewhere way back in my past) a National Award that I can return, because it allows me to be a part of a political movement initiated by writers, filmmakers and academics in this country who have risen up against a kind of ideological viciousness and an assault on our collective IQ that will tear us apart and bury us very deep if we do not stand up to it now. I believe what artists and intellectuals are doing right now is unprecedented, and does not have a historical parallel. It is politics by other means. I am so proud to be part of it. And so ashamed of what is going on in this country today. P.S.: For the record, I turned down the Sahitya Akademi Award in 2005 when the Congress was in power. So please spare me that old Congress-versus-BJP debate. Its gone way beyond all that. Thanks.[123]

---

[123]https://www.thehindu.com/multimedia/archive/02610/Statement_from_fil_2610040a.pdf, page 11, accessed 1 June 2021.

But they were not going to spare her of that debate. Roy, who had been vehemently critical of the Congress when it was in power, was also dubbed as a member of the Tukde Tukde gang, the invention of the BJP under Modi[124] to describe those who were attempting to hold on to the secular and diverse fabric of India. Many writers, scientists and artists who spoke out against the silence of the regime and expressed worry over the vitiated atmosphere that was building in India were discredited[125] and dubbed as a Congress sympathizer. It was ironic in the sense that the finest minds and the most reputed creative practitioners of the country had been sidelined in one go for merely pointing out the fears that were but a matter of everyday news cycle in India. The movement was motivated, they (supporters of the government and trolls on social media) said, and the motive was to tarnish the reputation of the Modi government.[126]

The Sahitya Akademi was coming under immense fire as more and more writers were joining the chorus. And still, it was under a strange pressure, or fear of sorts, to even mildly condemn the killing of a writer who had been awarded by the same autonomous body. At the peak of the movement, I spoke

---

[124]PTI, 'Modi govt to deal sternly with "Tukde Tukde gang" trying to take advantage of farmers stir, says Union minister Ravi Shankar,' *Hindustan Times*, 14 December 2020, https://www.hindustantimes.com/india-news/modi-govt-to-deal-sternly-with-tukde-tukde-gang-trying-to-take-advantage-of-farmers-stir-says-union-minister-ravi-shankar/story-4F2bycEKA4SLVD8eXO3QNO.html, accessed 14 June 2021.

[125]Ibid.

[126]Chandni Prashar, 'Anupam Kher's Anti-"Award Wapsi Gang" tweets leave Twitter Fuming,' NDTV, 29 October 2019, https://www.ndtv.com/entertainment/anupam-khers-anti-award-wapsi-gang-tweets-leave-twitter-fuming-1237693, accessed 14 June 2021.

to acclaimed poet Vikram Seth, who had not returned his award till then, to gauge his evaluation of the protest. His response shocked me, as it did to the readers on the following day. Without mincing any words, Seth, a globally renowned figure, made it clear that he expected better of the Sahitya Akademi and that he too would not hesitate to return his award if the Akademi continued to remain lip locked.

The Akademi award-winning author shared the sentiments of writers who had already returned their awards, noting 'it is for us to understand that although we refer to this institution as an autonomous body, in reality, this autonomy is limited to an extent and it seems to me that they are scared or there is some pressure'.[127] He came down heavily on those who were criticizing the returning of awards.

'There are many other ways, but the fact is that if an institution has either, through its action or inaction, not been true to itself or the people it is supposed to represent, then this is the most obvious and direct way to express one's disapproval.'[128]

The author of *A Suitable Boy* said he felt that the returning of the Sahitya Akademi awards could have been prevented if the Akademi would have spoken up in support of the writers.

'Let us see after this meeting whether they change their stance—whether they condemn the murders of Kalburgi and Pansare—whether they make a robust intervention or defensive statement. If they just silly shy and avoid taking a stance on the matter, whether because they are scared or because they do

---

[127]Saket Suman, 'You Cannot Fill the Ballot Box with Blood: Vikram Seth,' 20 October 2015, *The Statesman*, www.epaper.thestatesman.com/c/6952148.
[128]Ibid.

not feel at that place, then how can one respect an institution like that? I have yet not given up the award, I am waiting to see what the result of the meeting is,' he maintained.[129]

Amid widespread protests and return of the prestigious literary honour by at least 36 writers, the Sahitya Akademi on 23 October 2015 finally broke its silence, strongly condemning 'the murder of Prof. Kalburgi and other intellectuals and thinkers'[130] and urging the litterateurs to take back their awards.

The unprecedented marathon meeting held on 23 October 2015 in the capital was advanced from November under the increasing pressure of several writers such as Sahgal, Keki N. Daruwalla and Ashok Vajpeyi, who returned their awards and others like Vikram Seth, who threatened to return their awards if the Akademi failed to 'speak for' and 'represent' the writing fraternity and safeguard 'freedom of expression'.[131]

'As the only autonomous institution of Indian literature in all its diversities, the Akademi firmly supports the writers' right to freedom of expression in all the languages of India and condemns any atrocity against any writer anywhere in the country in the strongest of words,' said the Akademi president Vishwanath Prasad Tiwari after the meeting.[132]

---

[129]Ibid.

[130]Saket Suman, 'After 54 days, Sahitya Akademi Breaks Silence,' 23 October 2015, *The Statesman*, https://www.thestatesman.com/india/after-54-dayssahitya-akademi-breaks-silence-98935.html, accessed 9 June 2021.

[131]Saket Suman, 'You Cannot Fill the Ballot Box with Blood: Vikram Seth,' 20 October 2015, *The Statesman*, www.epaper.thestatesman.com/c/6952148.

[132]Saket Suman, 'After 54 days, Sahitya Akademi Breaks Silence,' 23 October 2015, *The Statesman*, https://www.thestatesman.com/india/after-54-days-sahitya-akademi-breaks-silence-98935.html, accessed 9 June 2021.

The emergency meeting of the Sahitya Akademi to discuss the alarming exodus of literary icons was attended by 20 out of the 24 members of its Executive Board. K. Satchidanandan (who had earlier resigned from all positions), Lalit Mangtrata, Prem Pradhan and Balchand Nemade did not attend the meeting where the body 'unanimously' endorsed 'the diligent and vigilant leadership provided by the president (Tiwari) to uphold the tradition and legacy of the Akademi'.[133] The resolution passed by the Executive Board also asked the governments at the Centre and in the states to take 'immediate action to bring the culprits to book' and to ensure the security of writers. 'Sahitya Akademi demands that [the] Centre and states maintain the ambience of peaceful coexistence in the societies and urges various communities of our society to put aside the differences on the grounds of caste, religion, region and ideologies,' the resolution said.[134]

The Akademi president, while addressing the media, said the institution belongs to the writing fraternity and is guided 'solely by writers'[135] and requested the authors to take back their awards.

The Akademi's resolution, however, comes after almost two months since the murder of Prof. Kalburgi (30 August 2015). The memorandum fails to explain why 'the only autonomous institution of Indian literature in all its diversities'[136] took 54 days to publicly condemn the death of a Sahitya Akademi recipient and other rationalist thinkers.

---

[133]Ibid.
[134]Ibid.
[135]Ibid.
[136]Ibid.

'The meeting of Executive Board notes that upon the assassination of Prof. Kalburgi, the president of the Akademi had telephonically requested the vice-president to contact Prof. Kalburgi's family and to convey the sense of pain and outrage felt by the Akademi.'[137] Several prominent writers, who have returned their awards, expressed their 'disappointment' at the 'self-congratulatory' tone of the Akademi.[138]

These were followed by reactions and counterreactions, but ultimately the movement died down. A popular opinion had already been created[139] that everybody who returned their awards or lent support to the cause did so because they were sympathizers of the Congress party and worse, they did not wish good for India. A frenzied atmosphere was created and the dignity of Indian intelligentsia was sent for a toss as ferocious troll armies ruled the corridors of digital media, hurling choicest abuses at the dissenters. Did they really have some evil intention in their mind? Or were they merely speaking out because the country was being torn asunder? One of the sanest voices of dissent at that juncture was Keki Nasserwanji Daruwalla, a leading poet, who had joined the Indian Police Service in 1958, becoming a special assistant to the prime minister on international affairs in 1979. He was later in the Cabinet Secretariat until his retirement in 1995 and was awarded both the Police Medal for Meritorious Service (1975) and the

---

[137]Ibid.

[138]Ibid.

[139]'Award wapsi to defame India: Anupam Kher leads march against intolerance protests,' *Firstpost*, 7 November 2015, https://www.firstpost.com/india/award-wapsi-to-defame-india-anupam-kher-leads-march-against-intolerance-protests-2498828.html, accessed 14 June 2021.

President's Police Medal for Distinguished Service (1985). He was awarded the Padma Shri in 2014. For his poetry collection *The Keeper of the Dead*, he won the Sahitya Akademi Award in 1984, which he had returned in protest against the Akademi's failure 'to speak out against ideological collectives that have used physical violence against authors'.[140]

When I asked Daruwalla why he had returned his award, and why despite the Akademi's strong, albeit belated, condemnation of the cycle of violence, killings and intolerance in the country, did he and other writers not take them back, he replied immediately stressing that he returned his award particularly because the Akademi did not do enough for a writer and, in fact, a Sahitya Akademi awardee (Kalburgi) was murdered. And he was murdered for being rational, for talking about so many things which fundamentalists of a kind did not like and because he was also pained at the death of Dabholkar and Pansare. He said that he did not take his award back because it was not a game of ping-pong. 'I did not take it back and I will not take it back and the institution I really blame is the Akademi. Kalburgi's family did not even get a condolence call for two months (from the Akademi) till the decision after its meeting when we held a silent protest march. So, I thought it was a bit heartless and also a bit craven on the Akademi's part,' he maintained in an interview with me, which was published in *The Statesman*.[141]

---

[140]Scroll Staff, '"Akademi has not stood up for beleaguered writers": Poet Keki Daruwalla returns his award,' *Scroll.in*, 14 October 2015,https://scroll.in/article/762194/akademi-has-not-stood-up-for-beleaguered-writers-poet-keki-daruwalla-returns-his-award, accessed 22 May 2021.

[141]Saket Suman, 'We can only throw back our awards', *The Statesman*,

I then asked Daruwalla why he felt there was a threat to freedom of expression in the country and his reasons for believing that a climate of intolerance was building up in India. He pointed to the murders of the rational thinkers, saying that these were proofs to cement his assertions.

He contended in the interview thus:

> A man was being murdered for his eating habits! But the (Union culture) minister, after Dadri, came out and said well, this was an accident. Very sad! And there were other statements by a number of people. For instance, Mr Amit Shah has said crackers will be burst in Pakistan if BJP loses in Bihar. I mean why are you doing this, what are you pointing to Pakistan for, that it is inhabited by Muslims? So, the mindset also, somewhere has to change, and this is very difficult for the RSS, etc., because they have been brought up with a particular ideology. But now people are saying we are being intolerant and they are being tolerant, they are saying this protest was manufactured. Ghar Wapsi and Love Jihad were manufactured, not Award Wapsi.

In retrospect, the Award Wapsi protest was the first major show of dissent against the climate that has now spread over most parts of India. Looking back from a time when all fears have taken their full shape, it is worth lamenting that the mere recognition of the writers' right as free thinkers to exercise their freedom of expression and voice their concerns over the state of affairs

6 November 2015, https://www.thestatesman.com/opinion/we-can-only-throw-back-our-awards-102169.html, accessed 12 May 2021.

in the country would have gone a long way. But instead of recognition, they were met with demonization.

Everybody who dissented came to be dubbed as an anti-national figure, they became members of the so-called Tukde Tukde and Khan Market gangs. One looked closer and found that all they were really trying to do was keep the country together.

They were carrying out their patriotic duties of speaking up against a regime that was increasingly refusing to bear allegiance to the secular and democratic credentials of India. They could have had it easy and not become a part of the movement that was going to subject them to such castigation because the protests surfaced barely a year after Modi rose to power, which meant that regardless of what they said or did, his government was still going to rule over the country for at least the next four years. It would be hypocritical to say that they were not against a party, ideology or personality. But they were also resenting the atmosphere that had led to such widespread vitriol, they were seeking the environment in which arts and literature flourishes, they were fighting to reclaim the India that they had been born in and the India that they had grown up in.

But the prime minister relished the limelight, used every opportunity to grab eyeballs and the media outlets went so gaga over him that they offered unprecedented time and space to further his reach.[142] As this happened, the habit of asking tough

---

[142]Punya Prasun Bajpai, 'A 200-member government team is watching how the media covers Modi, Amit Shah,' *The Wire*, 10 August 2018, https://thewire.in/media/narendra-modi-amit-shah-media-watch-punya-prasun-bajpai, accessed 14 June 2021.

questions was gradually obliterated from the mainstream Indian media amid several allegations of censorship and throttling of free speech.[143] A vast majority of Indians remained in the hinterlands and they were uneducated and underprivileged. They found the television channels spewing hatred and divisive agendas, but unequipped as they were, they took them at face value. Slowly but steadily, the definition of India changed. More and more people were pushed into trenches of agony while there was an equal upsurge among those who began to believe in divisive and communal politics.[144] Development no longer seemed to matter as many among Modi's core voters seemed to draw satisfaction from the suffering of their Muslim brethren.[145]

As days passed, the government's intentions became clearer through ordinances[146], assaults on civil society organizations[147]

[143]'Why does not the Indian PM Narendra Modi answer the questions of reporters?' ABP News, 21 July 2015, https://www.youtube.com/watch?v=3LfSxEQ2gsA, accessed 14 June 2021.

[144]Kunal Purohit, 'India struggles with religious lynchings,' DW News, 8 August 2018, https://www.dw.com/en/india-struggles-with-religious-lynchings/a-49950223, accessed 14 June 2021.

[145]'Bigotry in "Secular" India: It's 2018 and Our Social Media Timeline is Flooded with Islamophobia,' News 18, 21 June 2018, https://www.news18.com/news/buzz/bigotry-in-secular-india-its-2018-and-our-social-media-timeline-is-flooded-with-islamophobia-1782917.html, accessed 14 June 2021.

[146]First Post Staff, 'NDA takes the ordinance route: Narendra Modi regime outstrips UPA's pace but lags behind Nehru, Indira,' First Post, 20 September 2018, https://www.firstpost.com/india/nda-takes-the-ordinance-route-narendra-modi-regime-outstrips-upas-pace-but-lags-behind-nehru-indira-5223831.html, accessed 12 May 2021.

[147]Murali Krishnan, 'Why is India cracking down on human rights groups?' DW, 1 October 2020, https://www.dw.com/en/why-is-india-cracking-down-on-human-rights-groups/a-55105954, accessed 18 May 2021.

and appointment of unqualified Hindu nationalists[148] as bosses of India's top educational and cultural bodies. 'India's soul was crushed,' he said,[149] and reminded the Indian population that the entire country had turned into a jailhouse[150] during the reign of Mrs Gandhi. True, but the complexity in the manner that Modi attacked the Emergency lies in the fact that his deliberate references were coming at a time when he was himself being accused by many of engaging in similar practices.[151] He further used it to delegitimize the Opposition against his authoritative nature and the centralization of power.[152] So, India really found itself in a situation where people's liberties began to be snatched and every time the dissenters expressed their worry, the regime either outraged their modesty by questioning their patriotism and describing them as Congress sympathizers, or worse, they

[148]First Post Staff, 'NDA takes the ordinance route: Narendra Modi regime outstrips UPA's pace but lags behind Nehru, Indira,' First Post, 20 September 2018, https://www.firstpost.com/india/nda-takes-the-ordinance-route-narendra-modi-regime-outstrips-upas-pace-but-lags-behind-nehru-indira-5223831.html,

[149]"India's soul was crushed": PM Modi talks about Emergency in Parliament,' https://www.youtube.com/watch?v=1LyPjDpsDdI, accessed 12 May 2021.

[150]'India became jailhouse during Emergency: PM Modi,' India Today, 25 June 2019, https://www.indiatoday.in/india/video/india-jailhouse-emergency-pm-modi-1556038-2019-06-25, accessed 12 May 2021.

[151]India under "undeclared Emergency", says Congress after Modi brings up 1975,' Business Standard, 25 June 2017, https://www.business-standard.com/article/politics/india-under-undeclared-emergency-says-congress-after-modi-brings-up-1975-117062500406_1.html

[152]Pratap Bhanu Mehta, 'India's strong man: Narendra Modi remains an authoritarian at heart,' Global Asia, September 2018, https://www.globalasia.org/v13no3/cover/indias-strong-man-narendra-modi-remains-an-authoritarian-at-heart_pratap-bhanu-mehta, accessed 14 June 2021.

were dubbed as members of dubious gangs—Khan Market gang, Tukde Tukde gang, etc.—which the pro-government trolls invented.[153] And when the main opposition party expressed the same concern, the government's tone was to refer to the Emergency and suggest that they were the ones who had done it. The very fear that it could happen again was throttled with rhetoric every time it arose.

Understanding this complexity is tougher than it may seem on the surface. I am reminded of my interview with noted author and Princeton University professor of history Gyan Prakash, in which he clearly underlined what many feared to say aloud.[154] That the nation is embodied in the prime minister is the telling similarity between the Emergency of 1975–77 under Mrs Gandhi and the state of affairs in India under Modi; but unlike the former, Modi's 'authoritarian governance' is not based on 'the assumption of Emergency powers by the executive', said Prakash, who had just released his new book *Emergency Chronicles: Indira Gandhi and Democracy's Turning Point*[155].

Asked what made him reach this conclusion and what was

---

[153]Regina M., 'Nearly 18,000 Twitter accounts spread "fake news" for BJP, 147 do it for Congress: Study,' *The Print*, 31 January 2020, https://theprint. in/politics/nearly-18000-twitter-accounts-spread-fake-news-for-bjp-147-do-it-for-congress-study/356876/, accessed 14 June 2021; Pranav Dixit, 'Modi's political party creates abusive social media campaigns and breeds internet trolls,' Buzzfeed News, 27 December 2016, https://www.buzzfeednews.com/article/pranavdixit/bjp-trolled-indians, accessed 14 June 2021.
[154]IANS, 'Today's authoritarian power is far more ominous for democracy,' NewsClick, 23 November 2018, https://www.newsclick.in/todays-authoritarian-power-far-more-ominous-democracy, accessed 12 May 2021.
[155]Gyan Prakash, *Emergency Chronicles: Indira Gandhi and Democracy's Turning Point*, Penguin Viking, 2018.

its likely impact on Indian democracy, Prakash said that the two situations are not exactly the same, but both the similarities and differences are revealing. Modi's authoritarian governance, Prakash said, is by a combination of two factors.[156]

'First, the BJP government uses and abuses the centralising powers of the state to weaken institutions and stifle dissent by terming it anti-national. Second, unlike Indira Gandhi's Emergency, which never enjoyed popular support, Narendra Modi's government is able to deploy Hindutva forces on the ground to intimidate the Opposition. In addition, it enjoys support from the corporate media, particularly electronic media,' he said, recalling that there was no private electronic media during the Emergency, and the government-controlled media never enjoyed the reach and influence that the media does today.

'For these reasons, authoritarian power is far more ominous for democracy today,' he maintained. He said that the gatekeepers of democracy are its institutions—political parties, the rule of law, an independent press and avenues to express dissent.

He said:

You cannot realise democracy's substantive promise of equality without its institutions. Centralisation of power in one person or one office damages the health of these institutions. There were some people in India who welcomed the BJP victory in 2014 even if they didn't agree with its

---

[156]Covered in interviews. Also, IANS, 'Today's authoritarian power is far more ominous for democracy,' NewsClick, 23 November 2018, https://www.newsclick.in/todaysauthoritarian-power-far-more-ominous-democracy, accessed 12 May 2021.

Hindutva ideology. They thought that because the BJP was a proper political party with seasoned national and regional leaders, and not beholden to one family like the Congress, it would respect and strengthen democratic institutions. But the stunning depletion of its leadership to one oversized personality has meant that the space for the expression of multiple and divergent views in the party has contracted almost overnight. So has the possibility of the BJP playing its role, as a political party, as a gatekeeper of democracy.[157]

Prakash emphasized that the surge of Hindu nationalism has catapulted Modi into the kind of position that Mrs Gandhi occupied only with the Emergency. Asked if he was suggesting that there was an undeclared Emergency kind of a scenario in India, he said the term conjures up a false and misleading similarity.

Prakash explained thus:

The Emergency was a very specific state action, a lawful suspension of the law. But Indira's draconian laws and abuse of authority could never summon foot soldiers on the street to back her power. The very fact that she had to formally silence the press, meddle with the judiciary, and place over a hundred thousand people in prison were signs that her power lacked the force of popular support. The deployment of coercion to implement the 20-point programme, sterilisation drives, slum clearance campaigns, and efforts to break through the controlled economy, signified that all was not well with her regime at the

[157]Ibid.

ground level. This is why she resorted to the Emergency to salvage her regime and its policy agenda.[158]

He said the situation today is very different.

> Today we witness an unprecedented combination of state power and populist mobilisation in the name of development and the nation. Yes, there is a growing centralisation of power, and attacks on institutions, abuse of authority, etc., but what makes the current context radically different is that moves at the top are joined by mobilisation from below. This coordination between state and society—deliberate or not—threatens democracy in a fundamental way, one that is not captured by the term 'undeclared Emergency'.[159]

While many hearts were bleeding in India at the sad turn of events, and more so at the anticipation of the misery that awaited the country in near future, the regime sought to project itself as the liberator of India's poorest of the poor and hyped on its economic agendas through numerous hoardings, advertisements and repeated appearances on the television.[160] This was going to cost a whopping amount of the taxpayers' money, but Modi was showing a full-orchestrated cinema to the public and they

---

[158]Ibid.

[159]Ibid.

[160]Devesh K. Pandey, 'Remove PM's photo from hoardings, EC tells official,' *The Hindu*, 8 July 2017, https://www.thehindu.com/news/national/election-commission-asks-cabinet-secretary-to-remove-narendra-modi-photo-from-hoardings-in-goa/article17029438.ece, accessed 14 June 2021.

took them at face value.[161] They thought it was patriotic to support the government against the criticism from those the government was describing as anti-nationals.[162] Patriotism was at the heart of this cycle of propaganda, but it was depicted in a manner that patriots themselves began to lose their breath.

Then came the suicide of Rohith Vemula, after which came the gruesome murder of firebrand journalist and activist Gauri Lankesh and somewhere in between a student leader by the name of Kanhaiya Kumar was hounded and castigated for allegedly raising anti-India slogans. Everybody who questioned the regime, everybody who spoke up for their rights and the rights of their fellow countrymen, everybody who could decipher the sinister design, everybody who had the wherewithal to question the government was naturally sidelined and deemed even unfit to question. Arundhati Roy was already a celebrated traitor as hundreds took to social media on a daily basis to abuse and troll her although she was herself very much absent from the digital world.[163] But what had she really been arguing about?

---

[161]Ajay Singh, 'Narendra Modi's speech in Parliament: Behind emotion and drama was carefully-calibrated electoral strategy,' *Firstpost*, 8 February 2018, https://www.firstpost.com/politics/narendra-modis-speech-in-parliament-behind-action-emotion-and-drama-was-carefully-calibrated-electoral-strategy-4341551.html, accessed 14 June 2021.

[162]PTI, 'Anti-national groups using social media for propaganda: Ravi Shankar Prasad,' *The Economic Times*, 25 February 2015, https://economictimes.indiatimes.com/news/politics-and-nation/anti-national-groups-using-social-media-for-propaganda-ravi-shankar-prasad/articleshow/46370571.cms, accessed 14 June 2021.

[163]'BJP MP wants army to abduct, hold Arundhati Roy hostage to deter Kashmiri stone pelters,' *The Wire*, 22 May 2017, https://thewire.in/politics/paresh-rawal-human-shield-arundhati-roy, accessed 14 June 2021.

At the core of her writings, though ironic, she was raising her voice for the very people who were castigating her in the trance of the emperor who had shown them vivid dreams.

Actor and BJP parliamentarian Paresh Rawal, for example, launched an all-out attack on Roy in 2017. 'Instead of tying stone pelter on the army jeep tie Arundhati Roy,' the Lok Sabha member from Gujarat tweeted late on 22 May 2017.[164] While Rawal was referring to the controversial 9 April 2017 incident in Kashmir where Farooq Dar, a civilian was tied to the front of an army vehicle and paraded across at least nine villages as a 'human shield' against stone pelters, the context in which he targeted Roy seemed mysterious, at least for the first few hours. Rawal's tweet also mentioned a Facebook post '70 lakh Indian Army cannot defeat Azadi gang in Kashmir: Arundhati Roy gives statement to Pakistani newspaper!'[165] There was a catch though.

Award-winning journalist Ravi Agrawal, in his book *India Connected: How the Smartphone is Transforming the World's Largest Democracy*[166], later pointed out that communal tensions such as this have been sensitive to internet rumours. He highlighted that on 16 May 2017, a *Times of Islamabad* story claimed that she had insulted the Indian government in a speech, adding that

---

[164]'Why not tie Arundhati Roy to an Army jeep, asks Paresh Rawal,' *The Hindu BusinessLine*, 11 January 2018 https://www.thehindubusinessline. com/news/national/why-not-tie-arundhati-roy-to-an-army-jeep-asks-paresh-rawal/article9710008.ece, accessed 1 July 2021.

[165]'Paresh Rawal's tweet about Arundhati Roy triggered by fake news: report,' *Deccan Herald*, 24 May 2017.

[166]Ravi Agrawal, *India Connected: How the Smartphone is Transforming the World's Largest Democracy,* United Kingdom: Oxford University Press, 2018.

Roy had said the Indian army would be incapable of fighting in Kashmir even if it increased its presence there by a factor of 10.[167] While several Pakistani media outlets made a massive show out of that report, the Indian TV anchors too went berserk, with one calling Roy a 'one-book wonder'.

'No one stopped to do basic journalism. A quick internet search or a phone call would have revealed that the *Times of Islamabad* wasn't a real newspaper, it was a nationalist Pakistani site. Roy hadn't been to Srinagar in months. The comments attributed to her had been made up,' contended Agrawal in his book from Oxford University Press.[168]

They became so oblivious to the reality due to widespread propaganda and misinformation as a matter of deliberate political weapon[169] that without quite understanding the fears gnawing at the heart of the writer, they took to abusing and trolling her as if she was everything they had to deal with. As if healthcare, jobs, the economy and the poor did not matter. As if a writer's assertions were holding India back from marching onwards. As if she was the enemy of the nation and hunger, poverty and marginalization were not.

But she made immense sense to me. Sometimes, only she made sense. As if everybody else was hiding behind a veil, telling only things that could be comfortably said, and ignoring things that were against popular opinion. She said it quite clearly that

---

[167]Ibid.:134

[168]Ibid.

[169]Nikhil Inamdar, 'How Narendra Modi has almost killed the Indian media,' *Quartz India*, 12 March 2019, https://qz.com/india/1570899/how-narendra-modi-has-almost-killed-indian-media/, accessed 12 May 2021.

she was not at all surprised by the state of affairs in the country.[170] To her, those were expected. And that sent me on some kind of an interrogation of the national ideals and set in motion a quest to really decipher what it means being an Indian in this day and age, which have, through sheer luck, found their home in this offering. There is no false pretence in Roy. She says things as they are, or at least as she feels and finds them to be.

To understand Arundhati Roy, you need to understand Susannah, and to understand Susannah, you need to know Mary and Rajib, Kottayam and Ayemenem, Meenachil and *The God of Small Things*. You see, a nation is not a sandcastle built in thin air. A nation is made by its people, the people who become citizens. Likewise, patriotism isn't something superficial; it is an emotion, like love that makes Roy wail for this nation, like hatred that makes people abuse her with such ferocity. And while love and hatred are both emotions, like patriotism, they are only as much different from it as they are from each other.

---

[170]Based on an interview with the author.

8

National Interest

Wherever patriotism is a driving force, the issue of national interest comes to hold immense significance even though there may be very little clarity among the citizens over where the interest of their nation really lies. The reason is that the lives of ordinary folks in most nations are so full of misery that the issue of 'national interest' becomes a ping-pong ball that they are deliberately made to play in order to overlook their own grievances and work collectively towards what is dubbed as the common goals by the elites and the powers that be. If it were not so, they would bring down the mountains and tear across mighty rivers to call for their rights and claim the privileges that are otherwise enjoyed only by a handful. In the words of Hans Joachim Morgenthau, who was one of the major twentieth-century figures in the study of international relations, 'The meaning of national interest is survival—the protection of physical, political and cultural identity against encroachments by other nation-states.'[171] But is it just this that threatens the patria? The patria acquires its complete connotation after its relationship with the people is established, which is to say that the patria is a barren geographical entity—virgin and unspoilt—until a set of, or several sets of, people come together and owe their allegiance to it. That's how states and nations are born, though there is also no denying the fact, as explored at length in previous chapters, that a shared cultural history is also pivotal to the foundation of many modern nations. Be as it may, 'We the People' is the centre around which the priorities of the governments elected by us to govern our nations are meant to revolve and, therefore, while it is true that securing the safety and sovereignty of the nations are legitimately defined as national interests, it can also not be disputed that the well-being and prosperity of the people are equally at the core of the ideals that should, ideally, shape these interests.

But there is more to it. As British statesman and former prime minister Lord Palmerston noted, 'We have no eternal allies, and we have no perpetual enemies. Our interests are eternal and perpetual, and those interests it is our duty to follow.' Friends and foes thus, in most cases, are created because of the circumstances to secure the interests of the nations. Thus, we have seen time and again that bloody wars have been raged and huge amounts of taxpayers' money has been spent in securing these interests. At the same time, many countries have also gone out of their way to help other nations in their hour of need and grief. While

---

[171]'National Interest and International Interest Part 1,' https://prog.lmu. edu.ng/colleges_CMS/document/books/National%20Interest%20&%20 International%20Interest,%20Part%201.pdf, accessed 12 May 2021.

much of it is superficially done in the name of humanitarian aids, the interests of the nations remain paramount even though they may not be so projected in the public eye. The exact definition of 'national interest' differs from country to country and from person to person depending upon his/her understanding or view of the national priorities and circumstances.

However, there are some salient features, independent or inter-related, that lead to the formulation of national interests. Territorial integrity is supreme and every nation holds it significant to defend itself from external aggressions. It is therefore that sovereignty, which is also a salient feature of the Indian Constitution, grants the given nation complete freedom to take steps or make decisions without the interference of any external or internal power. Sovereignty is the signature that grants validity to the check of national interest. National interest, then, is also about the well-being of the country's population. This requires the country to grow enough crops and grains in order to feed its citizens, have enough resources to ensure that their well-being is guaranteed and so on and so forth. A peaceful and harmonious society is also a fundamental aspect of national interest because all other activities in the name of national interest would become negligible if the citizens of the country did not live in harmony with each other. Thus, countries aim to maintain law and order in society, which in turn, is dependent on factors such as equality and liberty because fraternity cannot be achieved without these two. It is beyond doubt that national interest lies in overcoming differences that citizens may have among themselves and in containing civil unrest and riots. Added to it is the situation prevailing in its neighbourhood, which implies that the national interest of one nation demands that there is regional peace and security because no nation can remain peaceful for long if countries with which it shares its immediate borders are not at peace among themselves.

At the end of the day, every nation, quietly or quite vocally, is engaged in a constant process of securing its national interests. Foreign policies are so crafted that they meet the well-defined objectives and interests of their nations and it is also a universally accepted right of each nation to do so. Nations have often used this quite ambiguous term to justify their actions and it really depends on the context in which it is used. For example: German dictator Adolf Hitler sought to justify and carry on with his expansionist programme in the name of national interest and that led to the most disastrous war humanity has ever seen. Mankind began to be at odds among themselves as men and women were killing their counterparts. That, as we now know, cannot be justified in the name of national interest because national interest is not the exclusive right of one nation; it is rather the privilege of all.

But national interest can sometimes be intertwined or portrayed to be so with the interest of the politicians and the powers that rule a given nation. As India began to show its lust for blood and went on a path that its founders had forbade, this became more and more apparent with the deliberate use of the term 'national interest' to suit every motive of the regime. And the route to evil passed through mesmerizing lanes where songs invoking the Mahatma and slogans hailing the brave patriots of India were sung and chanted again and again.

It would perhaps be apt to recall at this juncture that it all began with Modi's ambitious Swachh Bharat Abhiyan, a cleanliness drive that sought to free India of filth, dirt and garbage, matters of abysmal shame that had perpetually plagued the nation.[172] Wasn't it fascinating? What could be more apt than launching a cleanliness drive in the interest of the nation? And he did it with mega show and pomp, advertisements and the participation of leading social media influencers. Shashi, who had been elected to Parliament from the Thiruvananthapuram constituency of Kerala in what was a rather tough battle for the Congress at large, was among his chosen few to carry forward the message of swachhta, or cleanliness. Many had expected that Shashi, a hardcore Congressman and believer in the ideals and legacies left behind by Gandhi and Nehru, would turn down the offer made by the newly elected prime minister, who had allegedly rallied against the secular fabric of India at several occasions. The anticipation seemed similar among Congress workers and party high command, which is perhaps why he faced a severe backlash after hailing the cleanliness drive launched by Modi and promoting it himself in his constituency as well as on social media, where he enjoys a massive following.

As Shashi accepted Modi's invitation for the 'Swachh Bharat Abhiyan', he made it amply clear that he was surprised at the Congress's criticism over his participation in the movement.[173] He emphasized that while inviting, the prime minister specifically

---

[172]PM India, Major Initiatives: Swachh Bharat Abhiyan, https://www.pmindia.gov.in/en/major_initiatives/swachh-bharat-abhiyan/, accessed 12 May 2021.

[173]ANI, 'Shashi Tharoor cordially accepts PM Modi's invitation for "Swachh Bharat Abhiyan", says surprised at Congress' criticism,' *Business Standard*, 7 October 2014, https://www.business-standard.com/multimedia/video-gallery/general/shashi-tharoor-cordially-accepts-pm-modi-s-invitation-for-swachh-bharat-abhiyan-says-surprised-at-congress-criticism-12278.htm, accessed 12 May 2021.

addressed him as Congress leader and MP and went on to add that the campaign was in line with a goal aimed by Gandhi, towards which everybody, regardless of their political affiliations, should work together and lay collective emphasis on a sustained effort to take the programmes of sanitation ahead. Taking up the prime minister's 'Clean India challenge', Shashi joined locals in cleaning the Vizhinjam port. 'Vizhinjam is a splendid beach. We will not allow it to become a dumping yard,' he was quoted as saying by *Hindustan Times*, adding he would see that his initiative is followed up.[174] The urbane parliamentarian was soon removed from the Congress party spokesperson's post after he accepted Modi's challenge and thanked him for making him a part of the nationwide campaign.[175] It turned out that the Congress leaders in Kerala had complained to the party high command saying his praise of Modi demoralized party workers who worked against the BJP. Without mincing words, Shashi made it clear that he was proud to be a Congressman and an Indian and that India should be put first. He noted that cleanliness was a national concern and urged people that no political meaning should be read into his support to the movement.

That's how the first salvo of national interest was fired by the Modi regime. It was an experiment of sorts to gauge

---

[174]'Tharoor joins PM's "Swachh Bharat" campaign,' *Hindustan Times*, 25 October 2024, https://www.hindustantimes.com/india/tharoor-joins-pm-s-swachh-bharat-campaign/story-s5lP1tb3AdLnFpkZ61KzBK.html, accessed 12 May 2021.

[175]Anita Joshua, 'Congress drops Shashi Tharoor as spokesperson,' *The Hindu*, 23 May 2016, https://www.thehindu.com/news/national/congress-drops-shashi-tharoor-as-party-spokesperson/article6496843.ece, accessed 12 May 2021.

the reaction it would elicit from his political opposition. It was also a ploy; whether one supported Modi or denounced his newly launched programme, criticism was meant to follow. But cleanliness indeed was the need of the hour and when a government proposed to go out of its way to improve sanitation in the country, Shashi joined the movement with all enthusiasm. While the portrait of Gandhi was used to headline the campaign and a leading Bollywood singer was roped in to compose a song that would echo at much-touted public events by leading members of the ruling government, there were many who thought that the government was only engaging in paying lip service to the Mahatma.

Acclaimed historian and Gandhi's most famous biographer Ramachandra Guha says that he finds double standards in the respect that the BJP and its ideological parent, the RSS, accord to the Father of the Nation. Speaking to me in an interview for the Indo Asian News Service, where I headed the Arts/Books/Culture verticals before quitting, Guha said that the RSS particularly is very ambivalent about Gandhi.[176]

> When Gandhi was alive, the RSS actively disliked him. They were absolutely opposed to equal rights for Muslims. In their list of heroes, Gandhi ranks very low... Through the '50s and '60s, they paid very less attention to him and his teachings. From the late '60s onwards, his name started appearing in their programmes. There are clearly some

---

[176]Saket Suman, 'Double standards in BJP-RSS respect for Gandhi: Ramachandra Guha,' *The Quint*, 11 September 2011, https://www.thequint.com/news/india/bjp-rss-mahatma-gandhi-respect-ramachandra-guha, accessed 12 May 2021.

aspects of Gandhi's philosophies that are unacceptable to the RSS. And Mr (Narendra) Modi may have picked them up as an RSS worker. Today, he invokes Gandhi from time to time, but it is not clear whether it is instrumental, tactical, or a clear departure from how the Sangh Parivar views Gandhi. At best, I would say that the Sangh Parivar views Gandhi with ambivalence, and when he was alive, they did just the same. At the same time, they seek to diminish his stature by elevating their own heroes.[177]

Whatever the case may have been with the BJP and Modi's respect for Gandhi and whether one believed that their acts were genuine or not, the swachhta campaign was something that should have ideally drawn the nation together. After all, it was in national interest. That the country was extremely filthy and that sanitation was a major roadblock it faced were undisputed facts. But it took some time for the truth to come out as the citizens later learnt that a vast majority of the funds allocated for the campaign were actually used in massive PR campaigns[178] and what soon remained of it were pictures and videos of parliamentarians from the dispensation, such as Hema Malini, making a mockery of both the campaign as well as the people of India.[179]

---

[177]Ibid.

[178]Aroon Deep, 'Swachh Bharat spent Rs 530 crore on publicity in three years–but little on grassroots awareness,' *Scroll.in*, 22 November 2017, https://scroll.in/article/857030/centre-spent-rs-530-crores-in-3-years-on-swachh-bharat-publicity-but-has-little-to-show-for-it, accessed 14 June 2021.

[179]India Today Web Desk, 'Video of Hema Malini sweeping goes viral. After cleaning water, she is cleaning air, says Internet,' *India Today*, 13 July 2019, https://www.indiatoday.in/trending-news/story/video-of-hema-

Shashi's zeal was also short-lived as within a year, he found a mismatch between 'rhetoric and reality'[180] when it came to the steps taken to fulfil the goals of the cleanliness campaign. 'The government's words have not been matched by action for this drive. It should try to more meaningfully contribute in terms of resources, material and direction to the Swachh Bharat Abhiyan,' the former Union minister was quoted as saying by news agency PTI.[181]

There is no single definition of 'national interest'. However, it is understood vaguely as the major goals of a given nation. Just like cleanliness could be seen as one such goal, there were several other issues of similar importance that were going to bring turmoil in the lives of the people of India.

Our democratic tradition faced the first brunt of this onslaught. As a country that had gained its Independence after a prolonged struggle and had been led forward by the likes of Gandhi, a democratic way of life became inherent to the Indian people. If Independence was the beginning of a new era, the country learnt lessons from the Emergency and understood that its freedom could be at stake, not merely due to external aggression but also as a result of the rise of authoritarian regimes and the quest of politicians to grab absolute power and rule over the country like it was somebody's private property.

malini-sweeping-goes-viral-after-cleaning-water-she-is-cleaning-air-says-internet-1568328-2019-07-13, accessed 12 May 2021.
[180]PTI, 'Shashi Tharoor on PM Narendra Modi's Swachh Bharat Abhiyan: Mismatch between rhetoric, reality,' *Financial Express*, 12 September 2015, https://www.financialexpress.com/economy/shashi-tharoor-narendra-modi-swachh-bharat-abhiyan/134451/, accessed 12 May 2021.
[181]Ibid.

With the gradual but steady centralization of power by the Modi government, India's institutions that had been built with much care and fortitude began to shake and tremble.[182] The irony was no longer limited to the Sahitya Akademi but, in fact, every institution of the country that was controlled by the government was made to function in a manner that it either obeyed the diktats of the regime or would have to prepare itself for internal changes.[183] Non-governmental organizations that were critical of the government found their offices raided by law-enforcing agencies while all sorts of pressure was being built to contain any voice of dissent.[184] Amid this fiasco, Mr Prime Minister suddenly appeared on television one fine evening and announced that he was going to demonetize the country's high value-currency notes in one go. It was unexpected, and unimaginable too as 86 per cent of the country's currency in circulation was rendered useless

[182]'PM Modi takes centralisation of powers to new heights,' *The New Indian Express*, 13 March 2019, https://www.newindianexpress.com/states/tamil-nadu/2019/mar/13/pm-modi-takes-centralisation-of-powers-to-new-heights-1950437.html, accessed 14 June 2021.

[183]Akshay Balwani, AMP and Pradeep Chhibber, 'The power to centralise,' *The Hindu*, 17 December 2016, https://www.thehindu.com/opinion/op-ed/The-power-to-centralise/article14025225.ece, accessed 14 June 2021.

[184]Reuters Staff, 'India's federal police raid local Amnesty International offices,' Reuters, 15 November 2019, https://www.reuters.com/article/us-india-amnesty/indias-federal-police-raid-local-amnesty-international-offices-idUSKBN1XP1XT, accessed 12 May 2021; Vidhi Joshi, 'India accused of muzzling NGOs by blocking foreign funding,' *The Guardian*, 24 November 2016, https://www.theguardian.com/global-development/2016/nov/24/india-modi-government-accused-muzzling-ngos-by-blocking-foreign-funding, accessed 14 June 2021.

within four hours of the honourable man's announcement.[185] The decision was taken without the knowledge of key members of the government and against the advice of key economists. As soon as the announcement was made, television news channels touted the prime minister's move with sheer generosity and failed to show the courage to question the regime on both the legality as well as mechanism of the step that was going to plunge the country's entire population into unimaginable suffering. Some gleefully announced that the new notes came pre-fitted with microchips that would trace illegal cash hoardings and help the crackdown on black money.[186] Several others reiterated every word that the government said without really questioning the motives behind the step that actually turned out to be a massive disaster, and which would, in the long run, script the fall of the Indian economy that had blossomed under the able guidance of Dr Singh,[187] whom his successor had mocked in the choicest of words in the run-up to the elections and even beyond it.

Patriotism was once again the ploy that Modi exploited to give meaning to his ambition. In his sudden speech at 8 p.m.

---

[185]Zeeshan Aleem, 'India pulled 86% of its cash out of circulation. It's not going well,' Vox, 29 November 2016, https://www.vox.com/world/2016/11/29/13763070/india-modi-cash-demonetization-protests, accessed 18 May 2021.
[186]'No electronic chip in Rs. 2000 notes: RBI,' The Hindu, 2 December 2016, https://www.thehindu.com/business/Economy/No-electronic-chip-in-Rs.-2000-notes-RBI/article16440933.ece, accessed 12 May 2021.
[187]Vivek Kaul, 'Manmohan Singh vs Narendra Modi: The real India growth story,' Mint, 12 April 2019, https://www.livemint.com/politics/policy/manmohan-singh-vs-narendra-modi-the-real-india-gdp-growth-story-1555034270688.html, accessed 14 June 2021.

on 8 November 2016, the prime minister noted that in the past decades, the spectre of corruption and black money had grown manifold and told the people of his country that while India featured at the top in terms of economic growth, it was ranked close to 100 in the global corruption perceptions.[188] He, of course, did so after waxing eloquent on the policies of his government and blowing his own trumpet on the self-proclaimed achievements of his government.

He went on:

The evil of corruption has been spread by certain sections of society for their selfish interest. They have ignored the poor and cornered benefits. Some people have misused their office for personal gain. On the other hand, honest people have fought against this evil. Crores of common men and women have lived lives of integrity. We hear about poor auto-rickshaw drivers returning gold ornaments left in the vehicles to their rightful owners. We hear about taxi drivers who take pains to locate the owners of cell phones left behind. We hear of vegetable vendors who return excess money given by customers. There comes a time in the history of a country's development when a need is felt for a strong and decisive step. For years, this country has felt that corruption, black money and terrorism are festering sores, holding us back in the race towards development. Terrorism is a frightening threat. So many have lost their

---

[188]BS Team, 'Full text: PM Modi's 2016 demonetisation speech that shocked India,' *Business Standard*, 8 November 2017, https://www.business-standard.com/article/economy-policy/full-text-pm-modi-s-2016-demonetisation-speech-that-shocked-india-117110800188_1.html, accessed 12 May 2021.

lives because of it. But have you ever thought about how these terrorists get their money? Enemies from across the border run their operations using fake currency notes. This has been going on for years. Many times, those using fake five hundred- and thousand-rupee notes have been caught and many such notes have been seized.[189]

The oft-ignored fact is that the scale of his announcement was so momentous and so direct was its impact on the national life that most people failed to take note of smaller references in his otherwise lengthy speech. By stressing on the 'selfish interests' of those who, according to him, misused their office for personal gain and reminding the common people of the 'integrity' with which they lead their lives, Modi evoked a skewed sense of patriotism among his countrymen, holding the previous regimes responsible for corruption in India and suggesting that people of India were so full of integrity that they were simply being looted by those with vested interests. Although he did not mention it directly, it was abundantly clear that he was primarily holding the Congress party responsible for the ill of corruption. And then he shifted his focus to terrorism, another potent tool to weaponize patriotism. While he said that 'black money' was preventing India from marching on to the path of development, he also tangled the issue of corruption by suggesting that terrorists from 'across the border' were killing Indians and that they were being successful by using fake currency notes.

'…Honest citizens want this fight against corruption, black money, benami property, terrorism and counterfeiting to

---

[189]Ibid.

continue. Which honest citizen would not be pained by reports of crores worth of currency notes stashed under the beds of government officers? Or by reports of cash found in gunny bags?' he said.[190]

His speech was perfectly wrapped in a thick shroud of patriotism because if it were not so, the people of the country would have stood up and spoken out in disgust at how the legal tender, their hard-earned money and their savings could be made illegal. He made the people feel patriotic, he made them believe that by obeying his command they were doing good for their country. And, as we noted earlier, we feel patriotic when we believe that the government ruling us cares for us and works for us. That was the case with common citizens of the country who were still enchanted by his persona and who still believed that this man could sail them through.

But then he dropped the bombshell:

Brothers and sisters, to break the grip of corruption and black money, we have decided that the five hundred rupee and thousand-rupee currency notes presently in use will no longer be legal tender from midnight tonight, that is 8th November 2016. This means that these notes will not be acceptable for transactions from midnight onwards. The five hundred- and thousand-rupee notes hoarded by anti-national and anti-social elements will become just worthless pieces of paper. The rights and

---

[190]'Full text of PM Narendra Modi's address scrapping Rs 500, Rs 1000 notes,' *Mint*, 9 November 2016, https://www.livemint.com/Politics/wOGimcrwS8W6sdQzw1cymI/Full-text-of-PM-Narendra-Modis-address-scrapping-Rs500-Rs.html, accessed 14 June 2021.

the interests of honest, hard-working people will be fully protected.[191]

Note the use of the words 'anti-national', 'worthless pieces of paper' and 'honest, hard-working people'. The term 'anti-national' was naturally meant to reinvigorate a sense of national pride among the common citizens of the country, those he gleefully referred to as 'honest, hard-working people' and they were meant to rejoice that the wealth of the corrupt would turn into 'worthless pieces of paper', whereas all that was really going to happen was they were going to be robbed of their hard-earned money and made to stand in long, serpentine queues in order to validate the money they had earned in valid and legal tenders. Once again, the people of India were fooled in the name of patriotism because making the currency illegal could have been the easiest thing to do. As we noted earlier in this chapter, national interest, in the name of which demonetization was carried out, does not mean to bring the country's entire population on the road, but it instead lies in maintaining order and overcoming unrest. Demonetization broke the backbone of law and order and plunged the country into a state of utter unrest for several months and its ripples would be felt for long thereafter.

Mr Prime Minister went on to say:

Brothers and sisters, in spite of all these efforts there may be temporary hardships to be faced by honest citizens.

---

[191]'Prime Minister Narendra Modi's speech: Historic moment against black money in India,' *The Economic Times*, 9 November 2016, https://retail. economictimes.indiatimes.com/news/industry/prime-minister-narendra-modis-speech-historic-moment-against-black-money-in-india/55324058, accessed 14 June 2021.

Experience tells us that ordinary citizens are always ready
to make sacrifices and face difficulties for the benefit of
the nation. I see that spirit when a poor widow gives up
her LPG subsidy, when a retired schoolteacher contributes
his pension to the Swachh Bharat mission, when a poor
Adivasi mother sells her goats to build a toilet, when
a soldier contributes 57 thousand rupees to make his
village clean. I have seen that the ordinary citizen has
the determination to do anything, if it will lead to the
country's progress.[192]

He reminded the people that there would be sacrifices to be
made and there was nothing really wrong with it as patriotism
demands sacrifice whenever needed. But in this manner? Why
did it have to be the ordinary citizens who had to make the
sacrifice? Was it mere sacrifice, or an exploitation of their
goodwill when they were going to be made to stand in long
queues in the wake of an ill-thought-out policy? The poor
widow did not have to give up on her LPG subsidy, she was
poor and the purpose of the subsidy was to enable her to lead
her life; the retired schoolteacher did not have to contribute
towards the Swachhta campaign and the soldier who guarded
India's borders against all adversities needed to be rewarded, not
cut short of his income, and the poor adivasi mother did not
really need to sell her goat to fund the ambitious programme.
The government collected tax for that very purpose and if it
wasn't sufficient, it was the government's job to ensure that
it earned enough to fund such magnanimous exercises, which

---

[192]Ibid.

spent a bomb on advertorials and gala PR campaigns. The people of the country had elected his government for 'the country's progress' and not to be repeatedly put to test and forced to make sacrifices in the name of national interest.

Modi made it clear that it was a 'fight against corruption, black money, fake notes and terrorism'.[193] He dubbed it as a 'movement for purifying our country'[194] and asked the people to put up with difficulties for some days. 'My dear countrymen, after the festivity of Diwali, now join the nation and extend your hand in this *Imandaari ka Utsav*, this *Pramanikta ka Parv*, this celebration of integrity, this festival of credibility,' he said.[195]

That experience made us think of national interest more attentively than ever before. Wasn't it all right if we were undergoing some temporary turmoil for the greater good? Shouldn't we all make sacrifices for the well-being and prosperity of our nation? But whose well-being and greater good was it anyway? All one could see was hundreds of thousands of poor and devastated queuing outside banks and ATMs as if they were asking for alms and not recollecting what was rightfully theirs. The political Opposition alleged that the demonetization was timed to ensure that the BJP had its way in the upcoming Uttar Pradesh assembly elections, which it did, but more worrying were the news reports of money launderers and the rich converting their old currencies into new quite easily while the poor suffered.[196] The national interest of a

---

[193]Ibid.

[194]Ibid.

[195]Ibid.

[196]Ajaz Ashraf, 'Demonetisation tricks: The hair-cut that converts old currency notes into new,' *Scroll.in*, 1 December 2016, https://scroll.in/article/822966/the-

country lies in maintaining order and curbing unrest and here we were, in one sweep, the entire country was plunged into a state of economic chaos that it had hardly seen before in its history as an independent nation.[197]

About three months later, I interviewed one of India's leading experts on the black economy, who has studied, written about and lectured extensively on the phenomenon for nearly four decades.[198] Noted economist Arun Kumar, who taught at Delhi's Jawaharlal Nehru University (JNU) from 1984 to 2015, said that the demonetization design was flawed, the objective had not been achieved and there was a very real danger of the shortage of currency translating into recessionary conditions as the economy continues to suffer.

Kumar, who had played a crucial role in drafting the Janata Party's manifesto ahead of the 1989 Lok Sabha elections, said:

> While the objective of dealing with the black economy and terrorism has not been achieved, the economy is suffering. Any move to check the generation of black money should have been targeted at those who generate it without hitting others. It will not have any long-term impact on the black economy. Events in the last three months show that demonetisation cannot tackle the

---

hair-cut-that-converts-old-currency-notes-into-new, accessed 14 June 2021.
[197]'Why Modi's currency gamble was "epic failure",' BBC, 30 August 2017, https://www.bbc.com/news/world-asia-india-41100610, accessed 14 June 2021.
[198]IANS, 'Currency shortage could result in recessionary conditions,' *Business Standard*, 22 February 2017, https://www.business-standard.com/article/news-ians/currency-shortage-could-result-in-recessionary-conditions-117022200277_1.html, accessed 13 May 2021.

black economy since cash does not mean black. Hence, the design of the policy move is basically flawed. While the notes shortage will dissipate slowly in the coming months, the slowdown in the economy is not getting less. Thus, the problem is transforming from notes shortage to recessionary conditions in the economy.[199]

He was not the only one; in fact, most leading economists with experience and wherewithal were anxious on similar lines, but such a vitiated atmosphere of patriotism was evoked by members of the dispensation that even questioning the *note bandi* (demonetization) came to be frowned upon as an act of *desh droh* (sedition). It was done in national interest, to free the country of black money and terrorism, they said in their defence.

Shashi challenged the government's claims head-on. He described the demonetization policy as 'a monumental blunder'[200] in the context of short-term effects on the economy and also on individual human beings. He pointed out that some had even died of hunger and due to standing in long queues at banks.

In a *Times of India* article, he was quoted as saying,

There was only 4 per cent of cash to replace on the day of the announcement of demonetisation. It violates the solemn oath printed on the note that promises to pay the bearers by denying people withdrawal of their own money.

---

[199]Ibid.
[200]Kevin Mendonsa, 'Demonetisation a monumental blunder: Shashi Tharoor,' *The Times of India*, 21 January 2017, https://timesofindia.indiatimes.com/city/mysuru/demonetisation-a-monumental-blunder-shashi-tharoor/articleshow/56702447.cms, accessed 13 May 2021.

It is one disaster after another, (the government) started shifting from one goal post to another. First one wants to attack black money then you realise that black money turning white in banks, then start talk about counterfeiting. Ironically, terrorists are caught with new currency in their hands.[201]

In an article for Project Syndicate, Shashi wrote, 'Far from being a masterstroke, Modi's decision seems to have been a miscalculation of epic proportions.'[202]

That which we call national interest cannot be determined by one person, or one political party. You see, even though there is generally one party or a coalition that forms the government in India, there are different fields such as agriculture, economy, jobs, education, defence, healthcare and so on and so forth. If somebody claims to be a jack of all trade, he will, sooner or later, emerge as master of none. That is why we as a society have learnt to respect and listen to our heroes, and these heroes are not the ones who appear in movies or television series. They are experts in different fields—economists, scientists, doctors, diplomats and others of their kind—who gain mastery in their respective fields because they spend years learning, researching or practising them. That's why we know of Homi Jehangir Bhabha and Dr A.P.J. Abdul Kalam. That's how the White and Green revolutions became a reality and that is exactly how the

---

[201]Ibid.

[202]Shashi Tharoor, 'India's demonetization disaster,' Project Syndicate, 6 December 2016, https://www.project-syndicate.org/commentary/india-demonetization-policy-consequences-by-shashi-tharoor-2016-12?barrier=accesspaylog, accessed 13 May 2021.

foundations of modern India were laid. But not under Modi; he made his interest seem like national interest and exploited the patriotism of common people to carry out the devastating agenda that brought the nation's economy to a standstill.

It took two years for the institutional disregard that the Modi government showed to the Reserve Bank of India (RBI) to come to the fore. Noted economist and former RBI governor Raghuram Rajan sounded the bell. While speaking at the prestigious Harvard Kennedy School in Cambridge, Rajan rejected the claim that the RBI had not been consulted by the government before it went ahead with its decision to demonetize the country's 86 per cent currency in circulation.[203] 'I didn't ever say that I wasn't consulted (on demonetisation). In fact, I have made it quite clear that we were consulted and we didn't think it was a good idea,' he said, before adding that demonetization 'was not a well-planned, well thought-out, useful exercise and I told the government that when the idea was first mooted'.[204]

But no sooner had Rajan sounded the alarm bell that the pro-government news channels set out on a mission to discredit him by dubbing him as a Congress stooge.[205] And

---

[203]Yoshita Singh, 'Demonetisation was "not a good idea": Raghuram Rajan,' *Mint*, 12 April 2018, https://www.livemint.com/Politics/nr6wI4saRptCzldQYlvdxN/Demonetisation-was-not-a-good-idea-Raghuram-Rajan.html, accessed 13 May 2021.

[204]Ibid.

[205]PTI, 'Raghuram Rajan not Indian at heart, should be sacked: Subramanian Swamy,' *The Hindu*, 18 October 2016, https://www.thehindu.com/news/national/Raghuram-Rajan-not-Indian-at-heart-should-be-sacked-Subramanian-Swamy/article14324616.ece, accessed 14 June 2021.

then came the final words from Arvind Subramanian, the former chief economic advisor, who quit his post months after demonetization.[206] He described the move as a 'massive, draconian, monetary shock'[207] that accelerated the decline in economic growth.

When demonetization was announced, many looked to the bright side and believed in what the government claimed. But economists did not seem to agree. They contested the claims that demonetization would end corruption and put a full stop to terrorism. They said that the introduction of ₹2,000 notes would only worsen the situation and make hoarding of cash much easier. And that is exactly what happened.

Three years down the line, we saw that the Indian banking system as well as the economy was in the midst of a slowdown and an impending crisis.[208] Reports of banks being duped of thousands of crores and fake currency being seized in high volumes began to surface at an increasing pace. Hoarding of huge volumes of cash became prevalent and authorities were

---

[206]Ipsita Chakravarty, 'The daily fix: Arvind Subramanian's exit further depletes government's bank of economic expertise,' *Scroll.in*, 21 June 2018, https://scroll.in/article/883465/the-daily-fix-arvind-subramanians-exit-further-depletes-governments-bank-of-economic-expertise, accessed 13 May 2021.

[207]Scroll Staff, 'Demonetisation was a "massive, draconian, monetary shock", says former chief economic advisor,' *Scroll.in*, 29 November 2018, https://scroll.in/latest/903868/demonetisation-was-a-massive-draconian-monetary-shock-says-former-chief-economic-advisor, accessed 13 May 2021.

[208]Saket Suman, 'Over 43% unaccounted cash is in Rs2,000 notes. Did demonetisation really serve its purpose?' *India Times*, 21 November 2019, https://www.indiatimes.com/news/india/more-than-43-unaccounted-cash-is-in-rs-2-000-notes-did-demonetisation-really-serve-its-purpose-500869.html, accessed 13 May 2021.

struggling to curb it.

But guess what? The ₹2,000 notes, which were released by the RBI after the November 2016 demonetization of ₹500 and ₹1,000 banknotes, had become the favourite currency for hoarders. The information was shared by Finance Minister Nirmala Sitharaman in a written reply to the Rajya Sabha. She said that 43.22 per cent of unaccounted cash seized in the current fiscal year so far is in the form of ₹2,000 notes. In the first full financial year after demonetization (FY18), 67.91 per cent of unaccounted cash was made up of ₹2,000 notes. It was a bit lower at 65.93 per cent in FY19 and has come further down this fiscal. But this doesn't disregard the fact that almost half of the cash was still being hoarded in ₹2,000 notes, whereas the purpose of demonetization, which led to its introduction, was putting an end to money laundering and counterfeiting in the first instance.

On demonetization's third anniversary, Shashi took a jibe at the prime minister for his 'burn me alive, if I am wrong' remark. He sought an apology from Modi, saying that it is not the nature of democracies to burn people alive whereas an apology for demonetization would go a long way.[209] What was amusing by now was the fact that the same people who were hailing Shashi for standing up in national interest at the time of the Swachh Bharat campaign began to castigate and troll him for pointing out the failures of the government. Through his

---

[209]'Demonetisation: Tharoor seeks apology from Modi, says "democracies don't burn people alive",' *The Week*, 8 November 2019, https://www.theweek.in/news/india/2019/11/08/Demonetisation-Tharoor-seeks-apology-from-Modi-says-democracies-dont-burn-people-alive.html, accessed 28 June 2021.

books, *Why I Am a Hindu*[210] and *The Paradoxical Prime Minister*[211], Shashi challenged every false promise and betrayal that the Modi government had unleashed on the people of India. While in the former he laid emphasis on the nature of acceptance that is inherent in the religion he has practised devotedly all his life and how the religion was being maligned in the name of Hindutva, in the latter offering he drew his focus to Modi's own paradoxical nature and pointed out the difference between what the prime minister said and did.

'When I returned to India, I was not exactly unknown, people were aware of my books and writings. In fact, even when I was contesting for the election, my books had already been translated into Malayalam, so I was not an unknown figure here. But obviously, being in public life in India gives you an exposure and a visibility which is in a different order of magnitude. When I was living in the West, working in the UN and writing books, I was known to a certain segment. Now I am known to a much larger section of the population and therefore what I am writing these days gets a certain level of attention. It also happens that sometimes luck comes your way, when it comes to topics because when you look at something like *An Era of Darkness*[212], it was the success of my Oxford speech that made that book possible. To my mind, this suggests that when you and your ideas are a part of the national conversation, your books become a part of the national conversation too,

---

[210] Shashi Tharoor, *Why I Am a Hindu*, Hurst, 2018. .
[211] Shashi Tharoor, *The Paradoxical Prime Minister*, Aleph Book Company, 2018.
[212] Shashi Tharoor, *An Era of Darkness: The British Empire in India*, Aleph Book Company; First edition, 2016.

provided you chose topics that interest people,' he says in a personal interview to me.

All of this was enough for the troll armies and the supporters of the regime to create an image that could fit in their political narrative. And he was not the only one to face the onslaught of wrath. As we noted earlier in quite some detail, the fundamental characteristic of the Modi government has been its arrogance and the disregard it has shown to India's institutions and experts from varied fields.[213] The intelligentsia had faced the wrath soon after they spoke out during the Award Wapsi campaign. So, as elections drew closer once again, echoes of bullets and bombshells being fired across the Line of Control became audible to the entire nation. An exorbitant defence deal that had come under fire by the Opposition began to be looked at suspiciously as a leading newspaper claimed to have found evidence suggesting that the deal 'bypassed mandated procedures'.[214] These were unfolding at a time when the general elections was barely weeks away and India's otherwise vibrant press was facing several allegations[215] of censorship and coercion while most channels and regional newspapers had already

[213]Shiv Visvanathan, 'Undermining India's institutions: How the Modi regime ran one red light after another, *Scroll.in*, 28 December 2016, https://scroll.in/article/825022/undermining-institutions-how-the-modi-regime-ran-one-red-light-after-another, accessed 14 June 2021.

[214]N. Ram, 'Investigative reports by N. Ram on the Rafale deal,' *The Hindu*, 13 April 2019, https://www.thehindu.com/news/national/investigative-reports-by-n-ram-on-the-rafale-deal/article26447043.ece, accessed 13 May 2021.

[215]Hardev Sonotra, 'As Anil Ambani's Rafale seal soars, his news agency is being run to the ground,' *The Wire*, 25 March 2019, https://thewire.in/media/as-anil-ambanis-rafale-deal-soars-his-news-agency-ians-is-being-run-to-the-ground, accessed 13 May 2021.

succumbed to the regime. The mood of the election was being so shaped that there existed only one choice for India, and that choice was Modi, despite the assault on freedom of speech and expression, despite the assault on religious freedom, despite the rising wave of intolerance and despite the demonetization that had shrunk the country's economy.

But there was the intelligentsia, the watchdog of our democracy. And they stood vigilant, speaking out every time there was an assault though speaking out meant being subjected to threats and facing real dangers. By then Gauri Lankesh had been killed and the government hadn't even expressed remorse over her death let alone catching her murderers; Kanhaiya Kumar had been beaten up by lawyers in the premises of a court[216] and several leading journalists and writers of the country had been issued death threats. Several seasoned journalists had quit or were made to resign through direct and indirect means.

The architect of modern India and the country's first prime minister, Nehru, was being obliterated from the national discourse and even the Jawaharlal Nehru Memorial Fund, chaired by Sonia Gandhi and housed in the Teen Murti Estate had been served several notices to vacate the premises on grounds of 'unauthorised occupation'.[217] Nehru had deep affection and regard for literature and scholarship. The Nehru

---

[216]Saket Suman, 'Who's Cassius in Modi's Rome?' *The Statesman*, 24 February 2016, https://www.thestatesman.com/supplements/who-s-cassius-in-modi-s-rome-125887.html, accessed 13 May 2021.

[217]'Nehru Memorial Fund gets eviction notice, refutes "unauthorised occupation" charge,' *Outlook*, 24 September 2018, https://www.outlookindia.com/newsscroll/nehru-memorial-fund-gets-eviction-notice-refutes-unauthorised-occupation-charge/1389638, accessed 13 May 2021.

Memorial Museum & Library (NMML) in the national capital has carried on his legacy, but the centre of excellence became a subject of much controversy under the Modi dispensation. The Teen Murti Bhavan remained Nehru's residence for 16 years until his death in May 1964;[218] and barely six months after his demise, S. Radhakrishnan, the then president of India, formally inaugurated the Nehru Memorial Museum in November 1964. This faced intense criticism from, among others, former prime minister Dr Singh, who, in a letter, urged his successor Modi to 'leave the Teen Murti Complex undisturbed as it is' and reminded him that it is 'a memorial to our first Prime Minister Pandit Nehru. This way we will be respecting both history and heritage'.[219] The Opposition suspected that a plan was underway to change NMML into a museum of all prime ministers of India.[220] But Modi went on with his mission.

Around this time, Nehru's niece Nayantara Sahgal had already come out with a novel that had a rather unusual title, *When the Moon Shines by Day*[221]. She explained that the moon obviously does not shine by day nor does the sun shine by night. 'Something is wrong if one is forced to agree with such propositions, or be punished for refusing to agree,' she told

[218]IANS, 'What's fishy at Nehru Memorial? A timeline of its making and unmaking,' *The Quint*, 13 November 2018, https://www.thequint.com/news/hot-news/what-s-fishy-at-nehru-memorial-a-timeline-of-its-making-and-unmaking, accessed 13 May 2021.
[219]Ibid.
[220]Ibid.
[221]Nayantara Sahgal, *When the Moon Shines by Day*, Speaking Tiger Books; 1st edition, 2017.

me in an interview.[222] She contended that contemporary Indian history was being fantasized, the minorities were under threat and there was a long fight ahead to preserve the 'true meaning of India'.[223]

> In the BJP-ruled states, history is not just being rewritten. It is being fantasized. The Mughal empire is being ruled out of it. (Jawaharlal) Nehru has been wiped out of it. A fictitious narrative is being created in place of history, just as mythology is being promoted as science. The threat to the minorities and attacks on them, especially Muslims, and all others who do not fall in line with the ruling (party's) ideology, are destroying India's great achievement of unity in diversity and the democratic freedoms and equality that Indian citizens have enjoyed since Independence. We, for whom India is a secular, democratic, inclusive republic— whose citizens have grown up in freedom—can never settle for less, and the protests against the crushing of dissent and debate are coming from many different groups: Writers, historians, scientists, students, professors and Dalits. One cannot despair of an India that refuses to bow down to any form of dictatorship. But there is a long fight ahead to preserve the true meaning of India.[224]

---

[222]IANS, 'They are destroying India's great achievement of unity in diversity: Writer Nayantara Sahgal,' *Business Standard*, 3 October 2017, https://www.business-standard.com/article/news-ians/they-are-destroying-india-s-great-achievement-of-unity-in-diversity-writer-nayantara-sahgal-ians-interview-117100300347_1.html, accessed 14 June 2021.
[223]Ibid.
[224]Ibid.

And her fears came true on 8 February 2019 when the assault on free speech became visible to all.[225] Noted actor and director Amol Palekar was interrupted several times while speaking at the inauguration of an exhibition and asked to cut short his speech at the National Gallery of Modern Art in Mumbai.[226] He was speaking on 'loss of independence', but the regime's grip on India's cultural institutions and its fears of the Indian intelligentsia had reached such menacing proportions that it could not tolerate citizens with free and independent minds.

I dialled Nayantara Sahgal's number and waited for her reaction.

'It's becoming a habit of this government to stop people from speaking freely. It's not intolerance anymore, it is outright dictatorship. We have all seen how the Modi government has treated the creative imagination. They are not comfortable with it because they cannot control free thinking, they can only ban and prevent people from speaking. This is exactly how a dictatorship behaves. The first target is always the creative imagination. This government is behaving exactly like Hitler's Germany,' she told me,[227] before highlighting that just days

[225]Scroll Staff, 'Amol Palekar says he had asked National Gallery of Art director if his speech would be censored,' *Scroll.in*, 10 February 2019, https://scroll.in/latest/912722/amol-palekar-says-he-had-asked-national-gallery-of-art-director-if-his-speech-would-be-censored, accessed 13 May 2021.

[226]PTI, 'Amol Palekar's speech cut off at Mumbai event for criticising government,' NDTV, 10 February 2019, https://www.ndtv.com/india-news/amol-palekars-speech-cut-off-at-ngma-mumbai-event-for-criticising-government-1991122, accessed 13 May 2021.

[227]IANS, 'Not intolerance anymore, its outright dictatorship: Nayantara Sahgal,' *Outlook*, 11 February 2019, https://www.outlookindia.com/newsscroll/not-intolerance-anymore-its-outright-dictatorship-nayantara-sahgal/1476918, accessed 13 May 2021.

before Palekar was snubbed and interrupted repeatedly at a function for which he was invited, an invitation to inaugurate a literary festival to herself was revoked at the last moment.

'We are not going to allow this to continue and more and more people are determined to come forward and speak their minds out,' she said.[228]

To my mind, the ability to muster courage in the face of suppression, to cling on to India's inclusive nature, to give voice to those whose voices were being suppressed and to fight for the rights guaranteed to every citizen of the country by the Constitution adopted by 'We the People' was the supreme act in the interest of the nation at that point in time. Instead, our prime minister marched on to lay seize over all democratic, cultural and political institutions to fulfill his unending quest to remain in power by crushing dissent and demonizing critics.

---

[228]Ibid.

9

Road to Revolution

As these rapid transformations in the Indian way of life took place, 'a world too wide' began to make its appearance in both Shashi's life and the course of the nation that he serves as an MP. His 'big, manly voice' began to be criticized, ridiculed and targeted by the ruling dispensation under Indian prime minister Modi. The urbane parliamentarian's diction evoked suspicion among the members of the Indian Right wing as they repeatedly accused him of exaggerating matters. Although he had been targeted by his political rivals since his initial days in politics, things took an altogether different shape after the publication of *Why I Am a Hindu*. His assertion—that a vast majority of Indian Hindus share the same philosophy as him—found a huge number of takers, particularly among the reading circles. But why would he have said things like India will turn into 'Hindu Pakistan' if the BJP returned to power in 2019?[229]

In the run-up to the general elections, a major controversy brewed over Shashi's remark, in which he said that a Hindu Pakistan would be created if the BJP returns to power in the general elections. Here is how *The Hindu* reported it:

> At an event in Thiruvananthapuram on Wednesday (July 12, 2018), Mr Tharoor is reported to have said, 'If they are able to win a repeat of their current strength in the Lok Sabha then, frankly, our own democratic Constitution, as we understand [it], will not survive... because then they will have all the three elements they need to tear up the Constitution of India and write a new one.
>
> 'And that will enshrine the principle of Hindu Rashtra, that will remove equality for the minorities, and that will create a Hindu Pakistan... and that is not what Mahatma Gandhi, Nehru, Sardar Patel, Maulana Azad and great heroes of freedom struggle fought for,' he added.[230]

Even his own party, the Congress, asked him to be restrained after the BJP attacked him. Shashi, however, refused to retract, saying the BJP-RSS idea of a Hindu Rashtra remained the mirror image of the neighbouring 'intolerant theocratic state'.[231]

Maintaining that Hindus like him 'cherish the inclusive nature of their faith' and 'have no desire to live as our Pakistani

---

[229]Special correspondent, 'Shashi Tharoor kicks up row with "Hindu Pakistan" jibe,' *The Hindu*, 12 July 2018, https://www.thehindu.com/news/national/shashi-tharoor-kicks-up-row-with-hindu-pakistan-jibe/article24399540.ece, accessed 13 May 2021.
[230]Ibid.
[231]Ibid.

neighbours are forced to',[232] he added:

> I have said this before and I will say it again. Pakistan was created as a state with a dominant religion that discriminates against its minorities and denies them equal rights. India never accepted the logic that had partitioned the country. But the BJP-RSS idea of a Hindu Rashtra is the mirror image of Pakistan—a state with a dominant majority religion that seeks to put its minorities in a subordinate place. That would be a Hindu Pakistan and it is not what our freedom movement fought for, nor the idea of India enshrined in our Constitution.[233]

A day later, writing in *The Print*, Shashi made it clear that he feared the BJP would aim to change the Constitution of India. 'What is bizarre about the media drama over my remarks is that no one giving air time to multiple BJP voices frothing at the mouth about my words actually asked them one simple question: "Is the BJP giving up its dream of a Hindu Rashtra?"' he asked, pointing out that pro-government voices, from Governor Tathagata Roy to Union Minister of State Anant Kumar Hegde, have openly affirmed that.[234]

Modi and his men marched along with a populist agenda

---

[232]Ibid.

[233]https://www.facebook.com/ShashiTharoor/posts/i-have-said-this-before-and-i-will-say-it-again-pakistan-was-created-as-a-state-/10155962318898167/, accessed 18 May 2021.

[234]Shashi Tharoor, 'Shashi Tharoor: A "Hindu Pakistan" wouldn't be Hindu at all, but a Sanghi Hindutva state,' *The Print*, 13 July 2018, https://theprint.in/opinion/shashi-tharoor-hindu-pakistan-wouldnt-be-hindu-but-sanghi-hindutva-state/82782/, accessed 13 May 2021.

once again. A controversial biopic on the life of the supreme leader was due to be released in extreme close proximity to the polls, but it was blocked by the election commission. The movie, it said, 'has the potential to disturb the level playing field during the elections', and therefore 'should not be displayed' in any format until after the polls had closed.[235] But promotional material on the movie, including its trailer and songs that portrayed Modi as the saviour of the nation—'*main desh nahi bikne dunga* (I won't let the country to be sold)'—had already reached the people. As fate would have it, crores of Indians cast their votes in metropolitan cities, villages, islands and far-flung mountainous hamlets. And Modi, as *The New York Times* noted, 'won the biggest re-election India has witnessed in decades'.[236] He rode to power with an even greater majority, making him one of the most powerful leaders India had seen in its history.

According to a study conducted by the Centre for Media Studies, the BJP spent close to ₹27,000 crore in the election campaign.[237] In what emerged as 'the most expensive election anywhere', the BJP's expenditure was a whopping 45 per cent of the ₹60,000 crore.

---

[235]Adam Whitnall, 'India election body blocks release of controversial Bollywood Modi biopic as country goes to polls,' *Independent*, 10 April 2019, https://www.independent.co.uk/news/world/asia/india-election-narendra-modi-movie-release-bollywood-banned-a8863486.html, accessed 13 May 2021.
[236]Jeffrey Gettleman, Kai Schultz, Ayesha Venkataraman and Sameer Yasir, 'India Election gives Modi a 2nd term. Here are 5 takeaways,' *The New York Times*, 23 May 2019, https://www.nytimes.com/2019/05/23/world/asia/india-election-narendra-modi.html, accessed 13 May 2021.
[237]Scroll Staff, 'BJP spent nearly 45% – or Rs 27,000 crore – of total expenditure for 2019 Lok Sabha polls: Report,' *Scroll.in*, 4 June 2019, https://scroll.in/latest/925882/bjp-spent-nearly-45-or-rs-27000-crore-of-total-expenditure-for-2019-lok-sabha-polls-report, accessed 18 May 2021.

And the victorious leader roared:

… Friends, when the battle of Mahabharata ended, Lord Krishna was asked, 'Whose side were you on?' At that time, in the time of Mahabharata, the answer that Lord Krishna had given, today in the twenty-first century, in the 2019 elections, the people of India, the 130 crore citizens, have given the same answer as Lord Krishna. Lord Krishna had said that he was not fighting for any side. 'I was only on the side of Hastinapur,' he had said. The citizens of the country have stood on the side of India, voted for India. Therefore, this feeling of the Indian people is the guarantee of India's bright future. I have been saying from the first day of this election, no party is fighting this election, no candidate is fighting, no leader is fighting this. This election is being fought by the people of this country. Those who had their eyes and ears closed found it difficult to understand my words. But today, the people have expressed my feelings. Therefore, if there is a winner today, it is India. If there is a winner today, it is democracy. If there is a winner today, it is the people.[238]

He stressed that the election results were going to usher India into a new phase as he told the citizens that those who wanted a brighter future for the country had built a new narrative with this election for unity of the nation.

---

[238]BI India Bureau, 'Full text of Modi's first speech after historic election victory,' *Business Insider India*, 26 May 2019, https://www.businessinsider.in/full-text-of-modi-speech-lok-sabha-election-2019/articleshow/69467611.cms, accessed 13 May 2021.

He went on to say that:

The weaker section of the society has forced the country to reconsider their old beliefs. Now, there are only two castes living in the country and the country is going to be focused on these two castes. In the 21st century, there is a caste in India, the poor, and other castes in the country who have some contribution to free them of poverty. There are the ones who want to come out of poverty and the one who wants to bring people out of poverty. We have to empower these two. We have to walk with this dream.[239]

Every word he spoke was an expression of patriotism. Showered with flowers and amid chants of 'Modi...Modi', the re-elected prime minister's confidence was further emboldened. It appeared to most people that he was going to work on the lines that he was claiming in his speech. It was anticipated that with such a thumping majority Modi could carry on with the economic agenda and bridge the gap between what he referred to as the two castes—the rich and the poor—through 'sabka saath, sabka vishwas'. But this was a false hope and the promise, once again, was short-lived.

By now, we have explored various facets of patriotism and have delved deep into the issues that are in 'national interest' as opposed to outward displays and euphoria. For a country where tens of millions cannot read and write and millions cannot afford a wholesome daily diet, the priorities of the government rising to power with such a thumping majority should have been to liberate them from the trenches of poverty and usher

---

[239]Ibid.

educational programmes.

It is ironic indeed that Modi rose to power on the promise of creating jobs and economic opportunities whereas the country's gross domestic product (GDP) suffered its biggest blow due to demonetization and lakhs of jobs were lost thereafter, let alone creating new ones. It has also emerged that of about 72 lakh trainees under the Government of India's ambitious Pradhan Mantri Kaushal Vikas Yojana, a meagre 21 per cent was able to bag placements.[240] It was widely advertised and hyped eloquently upon, but a vast majority of those who enrolled under this ambitious programme of the National Democratic Alliance (NDA) government could not find a placement. Notably, improving the skills to equip trainees with the wherewithal to fit in the industry was central to the objectives of the programme, but only 15.23 lakh of the total 72 lakh entrants have been able to secure a placement. The revelation came at a time when studies suggesting the downfall in placements from top universities and colleges had become rife in premiere Indian publications and when the general mood of the business fraternity was hitting new low with every passing day. It is also worth noting that in its five-year rule till then, the Modi government had not rolled out any major educational programme that would benefit India's poor and guide them towards the 'heaven of freedom' that Rabindranath Tagore envisaged.

The Modi government, however, had different plans. The

---

[240]Saket Suman, 'Where are the jobs? 72 lakh trained under skill India but only 15 lakh secured placements,' *India Times*, 4 August 2019, https://www. indiatimes.com/news/india/where-are-the-jobs-72-lakh-trained-under-skill-india-but-only-15-lakh-secured-placements-372802.html, accessed 13 May 2021.

priorities of the government were very different from what periled the common men and women of the country and through the deliberate use of misinformation and propaganda,[241] it had succeeded, to a large extent, in doing what Indira Gandhi had done. For Modi's voters, supporting him, regardless of substance in his policy, became an issue of prestige and ego. They thought they were doing their patriotic duty while a sinister design was being achieved through the popular backing.

On 5 August 2019, Modi's right-hand man, Home Minister Amit Shah, while addressing the Rajya Sabha, proposed to partially scrap Article 370 that gave special status to the state of Jammu and Kashmir while a series of unprecedented events unfolded in the Kashmir Valley, leading to the imposition of restrictions under Section 144 CrPC in Srinagar district,[242] suspension of mobile and internet services as well as placing of two former chief ministers, Omar Abdullah and Mehbooba Mufti, under house arrest while the entire region came to be gripped in a state of utter panic. The Modi-led NDA government at the Centre pushed the Jammu and Kashmir Reorganisation Bill 2019 in the Rajya Sabha as Shah led his government in the Upper House with his signature firebrand oration to bring a complete overhaul in the structure of the northernmost state of

---

[241]Pooja Chaudhuri, '18 times BJP Spokesperson Sambit Patra shared propaganda-fuelled misinformation,' *The Wire*, 17 June 2020, https://thewire.in/politics/bjp-sambit-patra-fake-news-propaganda, accessed 14 June 2021.
[242]Saket Suman, 'A new dawn or the darkest day for democracy? India debates unprecedented uproar on Kashmir, sans Kashmiris,' *India Times*, 5 August 2019, https://www.indiatimes.com/news/india/a-new-dawn-or-the-darkest-day-for-democracy-india-debates-unprecedented-uproar-on-kashmir-sans-kashmiris-372867.html, accessed 13 May 2021.

India.[243] In the days that followed, the region was placed under complete lockdown with heavy deployment of the military, the internet was suspended and key leaders had been detained. The saga of curbing of liberties that began in 2019 has not seen its complete withdrawal even eight months later as I type these words.

There were all sorts of allegations and chest thumping. The country came to be staunchly divided among those who celebrated it as a historic step and others who alleged that by doing so India was losing its moral authority in the Valley. Arundhati Roy and Shashi Tharoor both opposed the move in their respective words and ways while there was no dearth of those who stood by the government too. For most Indians, however, it was a patriotic act that was carried out in national interest and that's where there is contention.

There can be no denying the fact that the region had remained a hotspot of trouble for decades and despite numerous attempts, a permanent solution could not be achieved. It is also equally significant to note that previous governments too had done what they thought was right and therefore, as the government in power, and through the approval of Parliament, enjoyed every right to do what it deemed fit. The arrest of key leaders from the region was also not something unheard of or something that had happened for the first time. The difference

---

[243]Saket Suman, 'Presidential order scraps Article 370 giving special status to J&K as Valley sees unprecedented lock-down,' *India Times*, 5 August 2019, https://www.indiatimes.com/news/india/unprecedented-lock-down-in-the-valley-two-former-cms-placed-under-house-arrest-mobile-internet-services-suspended-while-uncertainty-looms-large-372835.html, accessed 13 May 2021.

was in principle and the complete breakdown of democratic norms. While it is true that there were problems, India as a country began to say that it will reach a solution by alienating its own citizens. A nation is not merely a geographical entity; when people affirm their commitment to their patria, patriotism is born. Kashmir was blacked out of India and while it may be true that it had happened several times in the past, it was grieving enough that it was happening again, that India was becoming a controller of sorts without actually having the support of the people there.[244] The entire discourse of the nation was shifted to Jammu and Kashmir while pro-government channels carried out heinous propagandas day and night to brainwash the rural folks in the Hindi heartland.[245]

And this was going to do immense damage to the country's soft power. Despite the numerous challenges that India faced, it had successfully managed to portray itself as a country that was internationally revered and held in high regard. We may not have been the greatest economy on the planet, we may not have had the biggest army, but we aimed at winning hearts and wherever we went, we shared the glorious stories of our civilization. And we did not do so aggressively to challenge and look down upon others. It was always a soft power, remember Swami Vivekananda's historic speech in Chicago at the Parliament of

[244]Naseer Ganai, 'After The Nazis, BJP is the biggest propaganda machine: Omar,' *Outlook*, 6 November 2020, https://www.outlookindia.com/website/story/india-news-bjp-is-the-biggest-propaganda-machine-only-second-to-the-nazi-party-says-omar-abdullah/363740

[245]Ram Puniyani, 'Abolition of Article 370: Propaganda Versus Truth,' NewsClick, 10 September 2019, https://www.newsclick.in/Abolition-Article-370-Propaganda-Versus-Truth, accessed 14 June 2021.

the World's Religions? On the Kashmir front too, despite a sustained attempt by Pakistan to derail peace in the region, we always held on to our moral ground and were largely seen as the 'good'.[246] This image of India was now at the risk of being shattered as the reports sent shivers down the spine of the rational Indians and perhaps made them question if this was what their country stood for. The story of India had been told by the songs of Bollywood, hummed by Russians and the British long before India's rise as a world power. Our arts and cultural extravaganza, our writers and our philosophers had been the flagbearers of India in ways more than the duly appointed diplomats. Above all, we always held a moral ground. We stood for the right, cared for the oppressed and fought the good fight, at least we seemed to.

That same month, the United Nations human rights experts called on the Government of India to end the crackdown on freedom of expression, access to information and peaceful protests imposed in Jammu and Kashmir. Experts expressed concern that the measures would exacerbate tensions in the region. 'The shutdown of the internet and telecommunication networks, without justification from the Government, are inconsistent with the fundamental norms of necessity and proportionality,' said experts.[247] 'The blackout is a form of

---

[246]Saket Suman, 'Ripples from Kashmir can have implications on India's soft power. Can we please ease the air?' *India Times*, 11 August 2019, https://www.indiatimes.com/news/india/ripples-from-kashmir-can-have-implications-on-india-s-soft-power-can-we-please-chill-the-air-373298.html, accessed 13 May 2021.
[247]'UN rights experts urge India to end communications shutdown in Kashmir,' United Nations Human Rights, 22 August 2019, https://www.ohchr.

collective punishment of the people of Jammu and Kashmir, without even a pretext of a precipitating offence,' they added.

Besides, there was the psychological aspect of things that went almost ignored. While images of happily-ever-after scenarios were thrust against those of brutal force and suppression of protests in the Kashmir Valley, one may have been left wondering what was right and what was wrong, but whatever the case may have been, deep down all of us are humans and as humans we should have understood that two wrongs could not make a right. A painful memory lives in you for a long time after the deed is done and the day is gone. So, could we really afford to overlook the psychological dimensions of the Kashmiris who were forced to live under such a massive deployment of troops? Would the rest of Indians have liked it if the army was in their backyard in that manner? Would patriotism ever be the same again for the Kashmiris?

There was more to it and that was worrisome. The abrogation of Article 370 and the unprecedented events in Jammu and Kashmir unfolded at a time when there were some real urgent issues that the country needed to deal with on priority. Let us take a look at some of them before we really understand how patriotism can be used as a ploy to rob the people of their own rights:[248]

org/EN/NewsEvents/Pages/DisplayNews.aspx?NewsID=24909&LangID=E, accessed 13 May 2021.

[248]Saket Suman, 'Article 370 scrapped but these are 12 pressing issues in India that need immediate attention,' *India Times*, 6 August 2019, https://www.indiatimes.com/news/india/article-370-scrapped-but-these-are-12-other-pressing-issues-in-india-that-needs-immediate-attention-372972.html, accessed 13 May 2021.

1. The Indian rupee had declined the most in the preceding six years and it was showing no signs of gaining strength. The decline was the most since September 2013. Foreign portfolio investors, according to data from the National Securities Depository, had already sold a net ₹12,419 crore in equities while buying ₹9,433 crore net in debt securities in July while they had already sold ₹5,522 crore of equities while buying ₹755 crore worth of debt paper in August. People forgot that this government had come to power on the promise of reviving the Indian economy.

2. Indian entrepreneurs were really annoyed at that juncture. Several of them had publicly expressed their unhappiness at the manner in which they were being bullied by authorities and looked upon as criminals by the taxing and enforcement bodies. Founder of Café Coffee Day, India's largest coffee chain, late V.G. Siddhartha asserted that he was being pressured by a private equity firm and the previous director general of the income tax department, but those remained the last words of the entrepreneur as he died by suicide before people could learn more about the harassment.[249] At the same time, Kiran Mazumdar-Shaw, the billionaire businesswoman and head of Biocon, had just told a

---

[249]'View: Suicide of Indian coffee king VG Siddhartha should be a lesson,' *The Economic Times*, 1 August 2019, https://economictimes.indiatimes.com/news/company/corporate-trends/view-suicide-of-indian-coffee-king-vg-siddhartha-should-be-a-lesson/articleshow/70482923.cms?from=mdr, accessed 13 May 2021.

leading newspaper[250] that she received a phone call from a 'government official' who told her to refrain from discussing issues around income tax harassment. The government needed to do something to encourage business in the country. Instead, it chose to divert the attention.

3. There was a steep rise in crimes against women. A prominent BJP lawmaker had come under the scanner for not only raping the daughter of Unnao but also for using every possible means to throttle her voice. Our newspapers were full of reports of rape, sexual abuse and domestic violence. According to the National Crimes Record Bureau, in all, 3,78,277 cases of crimes against women were reported across the country in 2018 while the state of Uttar Pradesh, also ruled by the BJP, topped the list with 59,445 cases.[251] Deploying forces and doing everything the government could to curb atrocities against women in the country should have been the act in the interest of the nation at that juncture.

4. India's farmers were dying by suicide and as many as 10,349 killed themselves in 2018 alone.[252] But this was

---

[250]'Kiran Mazumdar Shaw says govt official told her not to discuss income tax harassment,' The News Minute, 4 August 2019, https://www.thenewsminute.com/article/kiran-mazumdar-shaw-says-govt-official-told-her-not-discuss-income-tax-harassment-106652, accessed 14 June 2021.

[251]Ananya Bharadwaj, 'Domestic violence top crime against women, sedition cases doubled in 2018: NCRB data,' The Print, 10 January 2020, https://theprint.in/india/domestic-violence-top-crime-against-women-sedition-cases-doubled-in-2018-ncrb-data/347814/, accessed 13 May 2021.

[252]PTI, '10,349 farmers committed suicide in 2018: NCRB,' The Economic Times, 9 January 2020, https://economictimes.indiatimes.com/news/

not all, they were also pushed out of the news cycle and their plight seldom found mention in the mainstream national discourse. The government had shown little interest in rolling out incentives or listening to their grievances. On the contrary, helpless farmers marching to the national capital to give voice to their problems were brutally lathi-charged and water cannoned across the Delhi-Uttar Pradesh border on the preceding Gandhi Jayanti.[253]

That was the real state of the nation at that point in time. There was an upsurge in agony. Despite the brute majority that the Modi government got, the problems of the people had not been solved. The government's job was to solve these problems and not create new ones as it did by its ruthless actions in Jammu and Kashmir. The country does not hold its rightful place in the hearts of its citizens unless it behaves so. If one's government becomes xenophobic and outright racist and has different definitions for different people, it will end up weakening the fabric of unity that binds the nation together. The fact is Modi chose the easiest thing to do; he did not muster the courage to win the hearts of men, women and children of Kashmir. Instead, he went on brutally, holding on to the land and alienating the very people whose commitment to the patria is the prerequisite for the birth of patriotism. It

politics-and-nation/10349-farmers-committed-suicide-in-2018-ncrb/articleshow/73173375.cms?from=mdr, accessed 13 May 2021.
[253]'Farmers march to Delhi turns violent,' *Deccan Herald*, 3 October 2020, https://www.deccanherald.com/national/breaking-farmers-march-delhi-695709.html, accessed 13 May 2021.

is no wonder that the definition of patriotism is very different in that part of the world, but differences could be overcome with love and gentleness if the government really had the heart to do so. It only showed its iron fist.

Conditions worsened. More jobs were lost. More people became helpless. More eyebrows began to rise. More students began to protest. More universities began to increase their fees. More businesses shut down. More public-sector undertakings or government-owned entities were put up for sale. BSNL, MTNL and Air India were all looking for buyers.[254] The RBI transferred the highest-ever surplus of ₹1.76 lakh crore to the government.[255] India's GDP continued to fall as did the Indian rupee. For a country that was already reeling under an economic downslide and lack of new employment opportunities, slumping sales of cars and motorcycles emerged as a new reason to worry as they triggered massive job cuts in the auto sector. News agency Reuters found out that many companies were forced to shut down factories for days and axe shifts. The cull had been so extensive, according to the Reuters report, that just the initial estimates suggested that automakers, parts manufacturers and dealers had laid off about 3,50,000 workers.[256] Meanwhile, mob

[254]Megha Manchanda, 'Sale of Rs 37,500 crore worth of BSNL, MTNL assets hits ownership hurdle,' *Business Standard*, 5 November 2019, https://www.business-standard.com/article/companies/sale-of-rs-37-500-crore-worth-of-bsnl-mtnl-assets-hits-ownership-hurdle-119110401305_1.html, accessed 13 May 2021.
[255]Saket Suman, 'RBI is transferring highest-ever surplus of Rs 1.76 lakh Cr to govt. What does it mean?' *India Times*, 27 August 2019, https://www.indiatimes.com/news/india/rbi-is-transferring-highest-ever-surplus-of-rs-1-76-lakh-cr-to-govt-what-does-it-mean-374457.html, accessed 13 May 2021.
[256] Saket Suman, 'Indian auto industry faces worst downturn, over 350,000

lynching was also being glorified and the most curious of them was the heroic welcome, with slogans of *'Bharat Mata ki Jai'* and 'Vande Mataram', of the seven persons accused of killing a police inspector in cow slaughter violence in Bulandshahr.[257]

Children were being fed only roti and salt as part of the mid-day meal scheme, but instead of doing a course correction, the journalist who reported the horrific episode was booked for conspiracy.[258] At the same time, while the working population of India was worrying about paying their monthly EMIs amid the economic downslide, a total of 2,480 cases of fraud involving a huge sum of ₹31,898.63 crore had rattled 18 public-sector banks between April and June 2018.[259] The ministers were evading

laid off but nobody is talking about creating jobs,' *India Times*, 9 August 2019, https://www.indiatimes.com/news/india/indian-auto-industry-faces-worst-downturn-ever-over-350-000-laid-off-but-nobody-seems-to-be-talking-about-creating-jobs-373110.html, accessed 13 May 2021.

[257]Saket Suman, 'Bulandshahr violence accused get hero's welcome as legitimizing mob violence is the new norm,' *India Times*, 26 August 2019, https://www.indiatimes.com/news/india/bulandshahr-violence-accused-get-hero-s-welcome-outside-jail-supporters-chant-jai-shri-ram-374361.html, accessed 13 May 2021.

[258]Saket Suman, 'Journalist who recorded UP schoolkids eating roti & salt mid day meal booked for conspiracy,' *India Times*, 2 September 2019, https://www.indiatimes.com/news/india/journalist-who-recorded-up-schoolkids-eating-roti-salt-mid-day-meal-booked-for-conspiracy-374861.html, accessed 13 May 2021.

[259]Saket Suman, 'While we may worry about our EMIs, Rs 32,000 crore bank frauds have surfaced within 3 months,' *India Times*, 9 September 2019, https://www.indiatimes.com/news/india/while-we-may-worry-about-our-emis-rs-32-000-crore-bank-frauds-have-surfaced-within-3-months-375367.html, accessed 13 May 2021.

questions and frowning upon criticism,[260] refusing to take any advice from stakeholders. So much so that an agitated finance minister Nirmala Sitharaman held the attitude of millennials responsible for the dwindling sales of cars and motorbikes.[261] They prefer to ride Ola and Uber, she said but forgot to mention that they were struggling to even find jobs and sustain their lives, let alone afford to buy automobiles. It had been three years since demonetization and despite the government's tall claims, fake currency, surprisingly, doubled in the country[262] instead of it ending money laundering, terrorism and corruption, as was the goal of the disastrous decision, for which the government had not even expressed a word of regret. In terms of severity of hunger, India had been ranked 102 out of 117 countries—the lowest ranked among South Asian countries and among BRICS nations—by the Global Hunger Index 2019.[263] The report noted that among infants aged six months to 23 months, only 9.6 per

[260]Sunil Prabhu, 'Union Minister ducks NDTV question on Kapil Mishra's hate speech,' NDTV, 26 February 2020, https://www.ndtv.com/india-news/union-minister-prakash-javadekar-evades-question-on-bjps-kapil-mishras-delhi-speech-2186045, accessed 14 June 2021.

[261]Saket Suman, 'Why millennials are way ahead in the game and #NirmalaTai got economic indicators all wrong,' India Times, 11 September 2019, https://www.indiatimes.com/news/india/why-millennials-are-way-ahead-in-the-game-and-nirmalatai-got-economic-indicators-all-wrong-375541.html, accessed 13 May 2021.

[262]Saket Suman, 'From ₹15.9 Cr to ₹28.1 Cr, fake notes in India nearly doubled post-demonetisation. Gujarat topped the notorious list,' India Times, 23 October 2019, https://www.indiatimes.com/news/from-rs-15-9-crore-to-rs-28-1-crore-fake-notes-in-india-nearly-doubled-post-demonetisation-gujarat-topped-the-notorious-list-378394.html, accessed 13 May 2021.

[263]Global Hunger Index 2019: India, https://www.globalhungerindex.org/pdf/en/2019/India.pdf, accessed 13 May 2021.

cent of them in India are fed a 'minimum acceptable diet'.[264] The pleas of the farmers against land acquisition had been junked while Bullet Train got a go-ahead into New India. The personnel of Delhi Police and lawyers were exchanging blows in broad daylight while law and order was left to the mercy of the gods. The national capital had turned into a gas chamber with the onset of winter due to air pollution. The price of the all-important kitchen staple, onion, skyrocketed to ₹100/kg, much costlier than petrol while the poor farmers were forced to sell it only for ₹8/kg to hoarders and middlemen. The agrarian crisis worsened further.

To cut a long story short, there was so much to do, so many problems to overcome, so many hungry people to feed, so many lives to look after, so many children to educate, so many crimes to prevent, so many patriotic duties to perform but the supreme leader came up with the Citizenship (Amendment) Bill (CAB), which became the Citizenship (Amendment) Act (CAA) to divert the attention of the general public from the issues that were really holding them behind.[265] This bill was also one of the core motives of the BJP and its ideological parent, the RSS. By amending the Citizenship Act of 1955, the Modi

---

[264]Saket Suman, 'India's priorities! Cow numbers increase by 18% while 90% kids go hungry,' *India Times*, 17 October 2019, https://www.indiatimes.com/news/india/cows-population-in-india-rises-18-per-cent-to-nearly-536-million-shows-census-378018.html, accessed 13 May 2021.

[265]PTI, 'Citizenship Amendment Bill an attempt by govt to distract people from its failures on NRC, economy: Congress,' *The Economic Times*, 9 December 2019, https://economictimes.indiatimes.com/news/politics-and-nation/citizenship-amendment-bill-an-attempt-by-govt-to-distract-people-from-its-failures-on-nrc-economy-congress/articleshow/72445274.cms, accessed 14 June 2021.

government hoped to provide a pathway to Indian citizenship for 'persecuted religious minorities' from neighbouring countries. On the surface, there was nothing wrong with it, but as the provisions of the new law became public, the bigotry of the BJP came to the fore. The law did not grant eligibility to Muslims and it was the first time that religion was overtly used as a criterion for citizenship under Indian law.

That's how patriotism can be used as a ploy and a political tool to retain authority and rule by misleading and distracting people through a deliberate mechanism of propaganda and diversion tactics. There were no foundations of a bridge between what he had referred to as the two castes: the rich and the poor, but instead the gulf was only broadening with every passing day.

Just as the bill sailed through the Lower House of the Indian parliament, voices of dissent and protests, which had already gained momentum prior to its introduction in the parliament, found further resonance in the north-eastern flank of the country.[266] An 11-hour bandh was immediately called in most north-eastern states of the country while protests began to emerge in other parts too. People from all walks of life, who believed that the bill would change the secular character of the Indian state, called for sustained protests even leading to a civil disobedience movement.[267] In separate letters and petitions, they asserted that

---

[266]Saket Suman, 'Guwahati becomes epicentre of anti-CAB protests, thousands hit the streets & defy curfew,' *India Times*, 13 December 2019, https://www.indiatimes.com/news/india/guwahati-becomes-epi-centre-of-anti-cab-protest-thousands-hit-the-streets-defy-curfew-502242.html, accessed 13 May 2021.
[267]Saket Suman, 'Launch civil disobedience against "divisive" CAB & NRC,

the legislation threatens the federal framework provided by the Constitution and will fundamentally alter the character of the Indian republic if it came into force. In an open letter, about 600 writers, artists, activists, former bureaucrats and ex-judges asked the government not to betray the Constitution. The signatories included historian Romila Thapar, author Amitav Ghosh, actor Nandita Das, filmmakers Aparna Sen and Anand Patwardhan, activists Yogendra Yadav, Teesta Setalvad, Harsh Mander, Aruna Roy and Bezwada Wilson, former Delhi High Court Chief Justice A.P. Shah and the country's first Chief Information Commissioner Wajahat Habibullah, among others.

The letter stated:

> All of us from the cultural and academic communities condemn this bill as divisive, discriminatory and unconstitutional. It will, along with a nationwide NRC, bring untold suffering to people across the country. It will damage, fundamentally and irreparably, the nature of the Indian republic. This is why we demand that the government withdraw the bill. This is why we demand that the government not betray the Constitution. We call on all people of conscience to insist that the constitutional commitment to an equal and secular citizenry be honoured.[268]

say ex-officials, authors & scientists,' *India Times*, 11 December 2019, https://www.indiatimes.com/news/india/launch-civil-disobedience-against-divisive-cab-nrc-say-ex-babus-authors-scientists-502107.html, accessed 13 May 2021.
[268]'600 writers, activists, ex-judges ask Modi govt to withdraw "divisive" citizenship bill,' *The Print*, 11 December 2019,https://theprint.in/india/600-writers-activists-ex-judges-ask-modi-govt-to-withdraw-divisive-citizenship-bill/333359/, accessed 14 June 2021.

The repression had reached its peak and it was time for revolution. Indians cutting across barriers came out in protest against the divisive act while members of the dispensation such as Home Minister Shah, who had openly sought to explain the chronology of CAB and the National Register of Citizens (NRC) to the general public now began to lie in broad daylight to state that the two were not interlinked.[269]

A Maharashtra cadre IPS officer said he had decided to resign from the service as a mark of protest against what he described as the 'blatantly communal and unconstitutional' CAB.[270] Abdur Rahman, posted as special Inspector General of Police in Mumbai, issued a statement saying he won't be attending office from the next day.

Alleging that the bill violated Article 14 of the Constitution and is against its basic feature, he said:

> This Bill is against the religious pluralism of India. I request all justice-loving people to oppose the Bill in a democratic manner. It runs against the very basic feature of the Constitution... The Bill is against the basic feature of the Constitution. I condemn this Bill. In civil disobedience I have decided not to attend office from tomorrow. I am finally quitting the service...

---

[269]Rohan Venkataramakrishnan, 'Who is linking Citizenship Act to NRC? Here are five times Amit Shah did so,' *Scroll.in*, 20 December 2019, https://scroll.in/article/947436/who-is-linking-citizenship-act-to-nrc-here-are-five-times-amit-shah-did-so, accessed 14 June 2021.

[270]Saket Suman, 'It is against religious pluralism': IPS Officer Abdur Rahman quits over Citizenship Bill,' *India Times*, 12 December 2019, https://www.indiatimes.com/news/india/ips-officer-abdur-rahman-quits-over-controversial-citizenship-bill-calls-it-civil-disobedience-against-blatantly-communal-unconstitutional-bill-502188.html, accessed 13 May 2021.

During the passage of the Bill, wrong facts, misleading information and wrong logic were produced by Home Minister Amit Shah. History was distorted. The idea behind the bill is to stoke fear in Muslims and divide the nation.[271]

This was patriotism fighting back and very soon more and more people were set to join the movement that would spiral across all parts of India and bring the country to a grinding halt. While these protests emerged, it became almost clear that the police was given a free hand to use force and brutality to crush this rising movement against the government.[272] There were reports of firing from the North-east while lathi-charge and water cannon had already become everyday episodes in India. Despite all repression, people came out in large numbers to protest because it was their nation they were fighting for. It was the set of principles that had held them together, and that fabric was being torn asunder. By excluding one religion from the CAA on one hand and by creating detention centres to cage people through the NRC, the Modi government's sinister design that the intellectuals, writers and artists had been long warning India about became visible to all. It was outright bigotry and communal politics. The agendas that were defeated in 1947 and 1950 were being forced onto India once again.

The government that had seemingly gained a PhD in 'Hindu–Muslim' politics sent its forces into the universities

---

[271]Ibid.
[272]'India: Deadly Force Used Against Protesters,' The Human Rights Watch, 23 December 2019, https://www.hrw.org/news/2019/12/23/india-deadly-force-used-against-protesters, accessed 14 March 2021.

and clamped down on students with brutality, leaving behind stains of blood and remnants of tear gas shells.[273] Jamia Millia Islamia, JNU and the Aligarh Muslim University faced the wrath of the authorities.[274] The students fought back with songs, slogans and graffiti. They drew caricatures of the supreme leader comparing him to Adolf Hitler,[275] and just as the government's repression became stronger, their tone grew sharper.

Comedian Varun Grover dedicated a song '*Hum kagaz nahin dikhayenge* (We will not show the papers)' that became the rallying cry of the movement. Faiz Ahmad Faiz was resurrected from his grave as his nazms and poems became relevant once again. This was Indian patriotism playing out in all its hues and as a reporter covering it first-hand at Jama Masjid, Jantar Mantar, JNU, Jamia and places beyond them in the national capital, one was overcome by all sorts of imageries that had suddenly been born in a nation that had seemingly been overtaken by fascist forces. The streets surrounding the universities were full of extremes—shattered glasses, bloodstains, remnants of tear gas shells and broken batons that the police used to clamp down on demonstrators.

---

[273]Saket Suman, 'Students launch immediate protest, citizenship law standoff leaves India searching for its soul,' *India Times*, 16 December 2019, https://www.indiatimes.com/news/india/students-launch-immediate-protest-citizenship-law-stabdoff-leaves-india-searching-for-its-soul-502424.html, accessed 13 May 2021.

[274]Saket Suman, 'Here's what happened with Jamia students last night and why cops are accused of atrocities,' *India Times*, 16 December 2019, https://www.indiatimes.com/news/india/situation-tense-in-jamia-millia-50-detained-students-released-502427.html, accessed 13 May 2021.

[275]Scroll Stuff, 'Citizenship Act protests: Five students arrested in Vadodara for objectionable graffiti,' *Scroll.in*, 18 December 2019.

But a closer look revealed surroundings teeming with hope, signs of a vibrant life—well-lived, well-read and well-versed with the law of the land. Orchestrated against the backdrop of the Citizenship Law were images and graffiti painted on walls and pavements, nooks and corners of the educational institutions that showed signs of a healthy protest. The images that then surfaced sent shivers down one's spine as they resembled the scene of a shoot-out or terror clampdown rather than that of controlling some agitating students and protesters against a law that had already attracted the ire of at least 500 prominent personalities from India, apart from being shunned by at least five states, and leading up to the carnage that was being seen in the North-east and the rest of India. These images evoked the popular opinion among the students that the regime sought refuge in the Indian Constitution to justify its actions, but failed to honour the true spirit of democracy and free speech, which the prime minister's 'holy book' entailed.[276] Some of the artwork took a direct dig at the prime minister, who infamously announced in the US, '*Sab changaa si*! (Everything is ok!)' in India. In response, the disgruntled students put up a graffiti of Modi dressed in a suit, embellished with the Nazi swastika.[277]

---

[276]Saket Suman, 'Hum honge kamyab, say protestors as Delhi defies prohibitory orders against Citizenship Law,' *India Times*, 20 December 2019, https://www.indiatimes.com/news/india/hum-honge-kamyab-say-protestors-as-delhi-defies-prohibitory-orders-against-citizenship-law-502672.html, accessed 13 May 2021.

[277]Saket Suman, 'Writing on the wall: Graffiti gets a rebellious edge in Jamia after police atrocities,' *India Times*, 17 December 2019, https://www.indiatimes.com/news/india/the-writing-is-on-the-wall-graffiti-has-a-rebellious-edge-in-jamia-after-police-atrocity-502514.html, accessed 13 May 2021.

It was noteworthy that these students could offer sermons to most parliamentarians on the Constitution of India, it was revealing that this was a young and vibrant India that was not going to be crushed and mutilated. It was encouraging that the country had an able generation awaiting. But it was disheartening that the government lacked humility and was drunk with ego and arrogance. It could even be understandable that it wanted to push through a bill that had long been in its agenda, but it was certainly not okay that it was overlooking its moral obligations of acting in the interest of the nation.

The government that was supposedly acting in the welfare of the Hindu population of India forgot to adhere to *'Raghukul reet sada chali aayi pran jaye par vachan na jaye,'* that one should not break one's vow, but here was a government acting in the name of Hinduism by openly violating and ripping apart the Constitution in whose name it had sworn and from which it had gained its authority. The Delhi Police's logo reads 'Shanti Sewa Nyaya' (Peace, Service, Justice). This message was lost when the cops clamped down on protesting students and barged inside the campuses. From thrashing students with torturous brutality to firing tear gas shells inside the university library, the Delhi Police marked a prominent shift in its action and behaviour by treating protesting students and dissenters at par with terrorists. As the death toll touched two dozen, India became an 'unsafe travel destination',[278] obviously causing more harm to an already dwindling economy.

---

[278]'Several countries issue travel advisory for India amid protests over CAA,' *The Times of India*, 17 December 2019, https://timesofindia.indiatimes.com/travel/destinations/several-countries-issue-travel-advisory-for-india-amid-protests-over-caa/as72835094.cms, accessed 14 June 2021.

While India continued to witness unprecedented protests and demonstrations against the CAA, Indian recipients of the prestigious Ramon Magsaysay Award too joined the chorus and expressed their outrage over the bill that they said was discriminatory and violative.[279] In a statement, they expressed their deep sense of concern and anguish at the passing into Law of the CAB and the linkage of the same with the NRC.

The signatories—Right to Information activist Aruna Roy, who received the Ramon Magsaysay Award for Community Leadership in the year 2000; Admiral (retired) Laxminarayan Ramdas, who was awarded the Ramon Magsaysay Award for peace in 2004; Bezwada Wilson, who was awarded in 2016; and P. Sainath, who was awarded in 2007, among others—said in the statement that:

> The act in its present form links religion with the question of citizenship for the first time in our plural, secular democracy, and is clearly divisive and therefore unacceptable. The outbreak of public protest and widespread demonstrations—some of them violent, does not augur well. The CAA and the NRC together have fanned the fires of earlier insecurities in Assam, the North East to entire India now—and there is an indefinite curfew and also shutting down of internet services in many states of the North East and elsewhere. Students in their

---

[279]Saket Suman, 'Indian recipients of Magsaysay award hit out at CAA & NRC, urge PM Modi to review the situation,' *India Times*, 23 December 2019, https://www.indiatimes.com/news/india/indian-recipients-of-magsaysay-award-hit-out-at-caa-nrc-urge-pm-modi-to-review-the-situation-502870.html, accessed 13 May 2021.

thousands are out on the streets—from all accounts with no political party affiliations or pressure.[280]

Modi and members of his government were doing everything possible to delegitimize the protest, to suggest that only Muslims were protesting and to brainwash his core vote bank into remaining oblivious to the real and graver challenges the country faced. In a remark that should have shamed the honourable position that Modi occupied, he went to the extent of saying that the protesters could be identified by their clothes.[281] He was obviously implying that only Muslims were protesting, but that was far from the reality. Other members of his party, such as Finance Minister Sitharaman, under whose watch India's economy was dwindling rapidly, had warned one to be wary of Maoists and separatists among demonstrators.[282] The reports of clampdown were increasing, but protests weren't showing any signs of dying down too.

Meanwhile, Shashi, through his speeches in Parliament and appearances on television, stood like a solid pillar and unending source of strength to the young and restless Indians. He was a Hindu, a respected MP and by his personal achievements, light years ahead of most of his colleagues in the historic building that is set to be turned into a museum now. So, why was he doing what he was doing? Modi himself expected Shashi's support on an occasion or two. Was he merely carrying out the agenda

---

[280]Ibid.

[281]"Can Be Identified by Their Clothes": PM Modi on CAA Protesters,' *The Quint*, 15 December 2019.

[282]'Must be wary of jihadists, Maoists, separatists getting into student activism: FM Nirmala Sitharaman,' *The Hindu*, 16 December 2019.

of his party? Was he exaggerating matters?

The most humbling lesson from Shashi's life is the fact that he has been consistent in his views. It is not like he has suddenly begun to to criticize the hard-line Hindu activists after the BJP's rise to power. Going back as early as the 1980s, he has been quite vocal about the nature of Hinduism he practises and believes in. With the rise of vitriol, sure enough, he became much more vociferous in his concerns. His writing is also nostalgic of the India of yore: the Bombay of his boyhood or the communal harmony of Calcutta when he lived there. For example: the concerns that he has been expressing in recent times found expression almost three decades ago in *The Great Indian Novel*[283], which talked about dharma and the significance of moral code in an individual's life; he has published a novel titled *Riot*[284], which is about Hindu-Muslim violence leading up to the Ram Janmabhoomi agitation; and in *India: Midnight to the Millennium and Beyond*[285], published 20 years ago, he described some of his core beliefs about the country.

'I was born nine years after Independence and certainly, it was a more idealistic time. In the India that I gained consciousness, which would be the Bombay of the early 1960s, was a very liberal cosmopolitan environment. My father had dropped his caste surname during the nationalist movement; he and my mother brought me up never knowing my caste until some kid asked me at school. I had Muslim friends, Christian friends,

[283]Shashi Tharoor, *The Great Indian Novel*, Penguin, 2014.
[284]Shashi Tharoor, *Riot: A Novel*, Penguin, 2015.
[285]Shashi Tharoor, *India: From Midnight to the Millennium and Beyond*, Penguin, 2012.

Parsi friends, Hindu friends and I never knew the difference, nor was I ever made to feel the difference by my parents. I mean national integration was not just a slogan; there was a very clear consciousness that if we had to be something better as a nation, then we had to aim at our own better natures and we had to overcome the recent bitter divisions of Partition. That was the India I grew up in as a child and, therefore, those are the values that I stuck with,' he elaborates.

These beliefs, he says, have been with him since a long time. 'But now I am living in an India, in which, unfortunately, we can't escape the purviews of arguments of the Hindutva version of Hinduism,' he says, insisting that Hinduism has been transformed into 'a badge of political identity'. And that's perhaps the reason why the otherwise humane parliamentarian turns feisty in his speeches these days. India, for him, is a lived experience that's being run to the ground and resisting it is the best shot he has to make his life worthy in the service of the great nation.

Arundhati Roy, on the other hand, is not a man. She is not an MP. And her experiences are different, as is her outlook and political ideology. But what had really happened, how did things go upside down?

'I had a dream the day after winning the Booker Prize. I was a fish in the river and someone just came and picked me out of the water, held me up and said I could have anything that I now wanted. "What do you want?" he asked. I just wanted to be put back in the water. Writing *The God of Small Things* and then winning the Booker Prize just blew my life apart,' she says.

When she was young Susie or even while she was studying architecture and then writing *The God of Small Things*, she could live in any way she wanted. The moment she became the first Indian to win the Booker Prize, her entire life opened up in the public eye. She was on the cover of every leading magazine and right when that celebration was taking place, the nuclear tests happened and one thing led to the next, making her an 'anti-national' figure. The state is of the people, for the people and by the people. At the heart of most of Roy's writing is a deep-seated interest of the people, whose commitment to the patria is a prerequisite for the thing we call patriotism. If there are no people, who would be patriotic? If there were no citizens, what would be the purpose of the country? Regardless, could she have done things differently, had the activist's gain been the writer's loss?

'It's not that simple,' she argues. 'I mean it is a great thing to write a book and to have the opportunity to speak. So, in a way I have also been warding off a constant process of domestication. They want you to write *The God of Small Things* II, III and so on. You are also looked at as a kind of asset that can keep that system moving. I don't blame them, but ultimately it is the writer who has to make the decision of what he/she is going to write about. I understand that publishers are also people who have to constantly embarrass themselves all the time by publishing books they don't want to publish, but they know that those books might become successful. And it keeps the industry moving. But then sometimes, a literary book, which also makes money, comes along and it gives everybody dignity. So, there is no need to feel morally outraged, but you have to keep doing what you have to do and not what somebody else wants you to do.'

Roy says that she has resented and spoken out her views

because of her belief in them. The biggest challenge, she points out, is never to look at them as mere issues because, according to her, we are all trained to separate them into little fragments and that makes everybody feel safer than we are, whereas our worlds are getting equally smaller with every passing day.

'To me, all the political writings is the accumulation of a particular kind of a political vision, at the heart of which I am constantly saying that while it may be true that every society in the world is unjust, are we a society that aspires towards justice or are we a society that is running in the opposite direction? Are we a society that institutionalizes injustice and has different standards to measure injustice for different people? To me, all the political writing that I do is to challenge that thought,' she asserts.

On one hand, she is received with grace and benevolence at foreign universities and institutions of repute, and on the other hand, she is viciously trolled and abused on social media. Several well-known and respected individuals have dismissed her assertions, but that is a right everybody has; things however take a different shape when a person, more so a writer, is targeted as an 'anti-national' force.

'To say that somebody who critiques injustice, who argues with policy, who looks at the way the poorest people or the most defenceless are being squashed is an anti-national, tells you what the idea of their nationalism is. What we miss in these times is any sense of fellow feeling, you miss politicians and bureaucrats speaking with real concern or love. Everyone just wants to hammer people with something on their heads. I don't sense kindness and love even in their talks, towards anyone...even the children dying in the hospitals,' she reflects.

It is the sad demise of love and gentleness—at the behest of skewed patriotism and extreme nationalism—that comes across as the most troubling feature of the current times for Roy. But how does she deal with all the vitriol that comes her way?

'When people called her names—clown without a circus, queen without a palace—she let the hurt blow through her branches like a breeze and used the music of her rustling leaves as balm to ease the pain,' she hints in the very first chapter of her second novel.[286] She says that she just ignores them, the trolls and those who call her names.

'You have to have a perspective on these things, you don't have to take them so seriously and put yourself at the centre of that story,' she says. 'It's alright that a lot of people are famous, but the earth is many hundred years old. So, if you don't think about it all the time and not place yourself at the centre of the narrative all the time, it's okay. I also think that I would be traumatized if a certain kind of person loved me. You have to wear it as a badge of honour. I mean if I was alone, then there would have been something wrong with my political thinking. Of course, I am not alone and that is what I keep trying to tell people, that the people who have the microphone in their hands and who man the television studios are not the whole nation or the voice of the nation,' she opines.

According to Roy's assertion, the idea of a country is a very recent thing, which she sees as 'an administrative union'. She points out that not so long ago, Pakistan, India and Bangladesh were one country or they were one country plus so many princely kingdoms. 'Then there is war, separation and

---

[286]Arundhati Roy, *The Ministry of Utmost Happiness*, Penguin India, 2017.

propaganda. Do we really want to be manipulated by such propagandas and talk about the foundational issues under such an influence?' She maintains that if she didn't have a very deep feeling for this place and engaged in 'a kind of love affair with the place that I live in', she would be living 'some antiseptic life somewhere else'.

'I never considered moving out. For me, this is my place. I love this place. The trees, the dying rivers, everything is here. I am not being patriotic, but this is my *mitti* (land)...the stuff that I write about, the stuff that I know,' she says.

Afterword

For how long can a mountain of lies bury the truth? Can propaganda and misinformation obliterate ground realities? We are told that the spread of a dangerous pandemic that left similar trails of devastation in many countries around the globe is the point at which the downfall of our great nation began. There are news reports, research papers and predictions that point to the pandemic for deaths, devastation and an economic downslide. We continue to pay taxes, wave the national flag, sing the national anthem and hail Bharat Mata because we as citizens are expected to behave as patriots.

Isn't this outright hypocrisy? Because the thing we call patriotism had very little place in our hearts when millions of our fellow citizens were left to the gods' mercy. If they somehow managed to defeat or escape the disease, hunger and poverty would surely catch up on them. Thousands of people were rendered helpless; many lost their livelihoods and watched helplessly as their loved ones suffered in front of their eyes. If we are still allowed to think freely, as patriots should, we will be able to read between the lines and learn for ourselves that our downhill slide had actually begun long before the pandemic broke out. It hit us when we were in our most vulnerable state, when our people were fighting against our very own Indians.

Towards the end of January 2020 when COVID-19 had just begun to attract eyeballs, we were already in a pretty bad shape. Protests and anti-government resentment had peaked as thousands would routinely hit the streets to point to the government's apathies and hold on to India's secular and democratic credentials. The Constitution of India gave them the strength, or so they said, while refusing to toe the line.

But then, the unexpected happened. Nobody really saw it coming. Within a matter of days, banners and flags were replaced by face masks and sanitizers just as newspaper headlines suddenly shifted focus to healthcare. People were advised to remain indoors, offices were shut down, transportation came to a standstill and only essential services were permitted to operate. Revolution became a thing of the past, a song only half sung.

Let us pause for a moment, if only to pay our respects to the fallen Indians whose lives we could not save during the outbreak. Were they any less Indian than those of us who survived and sailed through? Whose duty was it to look after them, care for them and provide them with necessary healthcare facilities? It is only when we begin to ask critical questions that we understand the true meaning and purpose of patriotism. People feel patriotic not only because of their attachment towards the patria but also because of the way things are in our societies. The nation is the embodiment of our collective spirit; it is like a family that is one in tears as well as in laughter. Just as ordinary folks are expected to adhere to the national ideals, to pay taxes and to work for national unity and integration, the country too provides a safety net that shelters its citizens and protects them when they can't really do anything to protect themselves.

When that moment arrived with the outbreak of COVID-19, India failed its people miserably or rather we failed India miserably. We left our country to the mercy of the gods, not because there was nothing that we could do but simply because of the constant derailing of the Indian thought process and the mismatch between what we said we would do and what we actually ended up doing. Our bureaucracy and the state machinery were so invested in misplaced priorities that it had lost its real sense of purpose and its ability to carry out the functions it was entrusted with. Added to it was the lack of a scientific temperament, the disregard for experts from varied fields, the centralization of power and our stinking habit of thumping our chests when so much remained to be done.

Remember, no stone will be left unturned to obliterate these deeply troubling traits from the collective memory of our people. It can very well be done in the name of patriotism once again. Do not question our government, or how dare you doubt the integrity of the honourable man? And you tell them, patriots are not slaves. They aren't meant to blindly adhere to a narrow and bigoted view of life. Patriots should behave as patriots, and they should call a spade a spade, a lie a lie.

While nations around the world were sealing off their borders and implementing strict protocols to contain the virus, India was preparing for a visit of the US president. On 24 February 2020, Donald Trump and Modi took part in a roadshow in Ahmedabad. The gala event for which huge preparations were made was attended by thousands of people at the sprawling Motera cricket stadium in Gujarat. The television news anchors roared at the top of their voices as the eager viewers cheered on in anticipation. Once again, it was hailed as a masterstroke by the supreme leader, whereas organizing such an event during an impending healthcare emergency was criticized for endangering the lives of thousands of ordinary Indians. We share the blame for not stopping Modi, for cheering him on and for celebrating that occasion, which was the first in a series of blunders India made in its fight against the pandemic.

This was our priority at that crucial juncture when all our effort should have really gone into containing the virus and assuring the dignity of our people. The response to a health emergency such as this was so vague and amateur in the crucial initial days that the devastation which the virus was unleashing in other parts of the world soon became a reality here too. When the situation began to slip out of our hands, a nationwide lockdown was declared, with a mere four-hour notice to the people of India.

Like swarms of bees, poor and devastated migrants living in the sprawling metropolis of India oozed out on the streets. Trains and buses were nowhere to be seen, highways were sealed off and security personnel were deployed in large numbers to maintain 'order'. The migrants were robbed of all their dignity, forced to walk hundreds of kilometres to their far-flung villages with nothing to eat and nobody to really call for help. Who were those people? We had only seen them in fractions here and there, working at construction sites or living in slums. An unimaginable exodus followed, but its reverberating boom fell on deaf ears. The country was officially dead to them; they had to do what they had to do for themselves and their families and friends. Labourers, construction workers, rickshaw pullers, taxi drivers and others who seemingly didn't matter in the national scheme of things began streaming out of the cities on foot, carrying their belongings on their heads, children in their arms and the fear of the uncertain journey in their eyes. The disease would kill them later, they asserted, but hunger would swallow them much sooner.

One of the first things that was carried out after the entire nation was put under lockdown was the deliberate painting of walls that, until yesterday, wore slogans and graffiti of protests. The regime thought that it could obliterate the memories of resounding demonstrations, it could whither the anger of the public and reinstil a sense of pride in the supreme leader.

Many couldn't make it to their homes. Some died on their way, were killed in accidents, were run down on railway tracks or were caught and apprehended on the state borders before being sent back to the city slums and containment facilities where, supposedly, preparations would be made to ferry them back to their villages.

The rest managed to pass through the gates of hell and reach their villages. Although they didn't see it that way, the disease had a very different definition back in the rural regions of Uttar Pradesh and Bihar. The Muslims were responsible for transmitting the disease; they were the carriers and should be boycotted was the irrational sentiment that had been provoked in the hinterlands. So, Muslim vegetable vendors began to be attacked, their shops were picketed and open calls of boycotting the very citizens of India by Indians were raised.[287] The fight against the pandemic became futile because the invisible enemy that the virus was began to be considered as residing in all Muslims of India. This drama would go on for weeks when news anchors raised their voices and spewed venom, in the midst of a health emergency, while Indian hospitals gradually began to be crammed. By the time people really understood that they were not each other's enemy but instead had a common adversary to fight against, the damage was already done.

As days passed, horrific stories began to emerge from city hospitals. Doctors and nurses suddenly became national heroes while innocent migrants continued to retreat to the hinterlands. A Bollywood actor and a Michelin-star chef set out on a tiring mission to provide them with food and assist in travelling. A footwear brand announced that they would provide free slippers to migrants. A young girl made it to the headlines after riding a bicycle from Delhi to her village in Bihar.

The earth continues to spin and our lives will go on. But we can make hay while the sun shines and set our priorities right. It is only when there is harmony and a sense of belonging that a country, state or civilization progresses. These are not the best of times to be optimistic. These are not the best of times to be nostalgic, but patriotism asks of us to cherish our freedom and to honour its sanctity by remembering how we became us

---

[287]Lauren Frayer, 'Blamed for Coronavirus Outbreak, Muslims in India come under attack,' NPR, 23 April 2020, https://www.npr.org/2020/04/23/839980029/blamed-for-coronavirus-outbreak-muslims-in-india-come-under-attack, accessed 14 June 2020; 'In India, Coronavirus fans religious hatred,' *The New York Times*, 12 April 2020, https://www.nytimes.com/2020/04/12/world/asia/india-coronavirus-muslims-bigotry.html, accessed 14 June 2021.

and how we lived our lives in the larger course of the nation. We have landed in a phase where we need to look back and identify the reasons why we went wrong. We must introspect and ask ourselves how we let our people down. We should stop concealing stories of our failures, lies and deceptions because patriots are not hypocrites. If patriotism is the affection of the people for their country, we need to look at and appreciate the things that bind us in this common thread. And we should hone and cherish the courage that it takes to speak up for the national ideals while recognizing the service of those who have done so at considerable cost to themselves. Slowly, the haze clears and the epic goddess of India reveals itself to us in quite a different avatar. It is on this promise that we have come thus far, our hearts beat against our breaths as we affirm our will to march onwards in its light.

But isn't that the colonization of our minds once again? Like innocent children sing their school songs and build up vivid imaginations in their heads about how their school is the best school that there is and why they should worship its rules like a religion. Isn't that how they tamed our minds when we were young? So, on a far greater level, mankind, as a species, will need to realize that the most complex challenges it faces are common. It is a different story altogether that despite this, patriotism worldwide is being manipulated to arouse fights and confusions among nations. Often, it is done to suit local political and vested interests. Can we move from this absurd culture of competitions and rivalries to an era of co-operation among countries? One can love one's country just as much as he/she loves the planet that is home to us all. Can we establish a similar relationship with the world we live in? Our planet has been ravaged not only by a pandemic but also due to rising temperatures, melting glaciers and natural disasters. Can we combine strengths of all our countries that are otherwise racing against each other and work collectively for a shared future?

Liberty and equality give patriotism its authority. Somebody who is not faced with unreasonable restrictions and is treated equally is more likely to feel patriotic than those whose voices are throttled and who have been marginalized by our society since centuries. Patriotism means different things to different people because in our society, we have different standards of judging people.

And it's not okay that we are not living in a world where everything is right and set to the tune of equity. But setting it right, fixing things and setting high ideals for a shared future of mankind are things we can surely do. We can become one as humans while being proud citizens of our varied nations, cultures and civilizations. We can prepare for greater challenges with as much vigour as we are expected to work for national integration. We can respect our people, each other, and believe that all are equal in our nations and all nations in the world are equal. When there is equality in and among all nations, there will be harmony in the planet. When there is harmony in the planet, patriotism will drive our zeal to find solutions to mankind's gravest problems, to address inequality and give everybody the dignity of our shared evolution from apes to humans.

Until then, patriotism will remain a sham, an invisible moral authority that prevents us from seeing that there are greater things at play, that there are deep states, the corporation and the powers that be, those that do not go away with the fall of governments or uprisings of the people. They are always there.

So, we need to become smart too. We should not hold ourselves back from asking questions about who they are and how they operate. We should start looking into political funding through electoral bonds more seriously. We should be cautious of the judiciary and detest its control, manipulation or misuse in any form whatsoever. We should believe in mankind's curiosity and the natural urge to ask questions, so we should celebrate the freedom of speech, press and expression. We should be mindful that we as people, people as nations and nations as the planet are vulnerable. At every stage, there are little things that matter. When we recognize and respect the presence of common challenges, we start working towards a world where all nations and people are equal. When we begin to aspire for that shared vision, the spirit of patriotism will become one for the entire planet.

We need to see through narrow domestic walls. The governments will always be there, as will states and nations in some essential form, but we as people need to think of the issues that are really plaguing our lives. Are people in countries where they earn more, more patriotic than the people in countries where they earn less for similar work? Or are they simply better off, better off as people but not as countries because even there, there is inequality? We should understand that regardless of the differences among countries in their historical occurrences and societal beliefs, patriotism is pro-people everywhere in a way that it empowers their collective strength.

We as a nation have been robbed of our power by a handful of wealthy oligarchs who use their power and position to trap our collective patriotism in the interest of a given leader. At every level of our electoral system, there is a massive pouring in of wealth. This is done to attain a position of power. Patriotism is the fuel that keeps this engine running, but then the undeserving politician begins to work for the corporations and oligarchs that have helped him attain power and loses sight of public interest. That is how we are robbed of our power, that is how our patriotism is trapped in a bubble and that is how we the people have once again become helpless in our own country and under the watch of the very leaders we have elected.

We should aim for an equitable and just society, but at present, we have the most massive misappropriate sharing in terms of wealth, where the top one per cent of us have more than the rest 99 per cent combined. This vast accumulation of wealth and building up of mega corporations and key players of the global economy is a result of power, which is essentially the position one commands in society. It is the instrument with which one individual rides over the rest. In its quest are most heroic stories born, but its very attainment denotes the superiority of one over the rest.

First, we established these with fights, battles and wars but then understood that it is money that does all the talking and went after money, bringing nuclear weapons, drones, advanced missile systems and other bombs into our backyards. When nations were born, they became the new corridors of power, but the tussle did not end there; it continues even till this day as every nation is constantly engaged in achieving its national interest and these quite often overlap among nations which leads to confrontations, disputes and alarming situations. Second, within nations we have centres of power in terms of political parties, populist leaders, monarchs and outright dictators. Patriotism is the instrument that enables the attainment of power. When people are sold to their ideas, the ordinary becomes a leader. Third, money never really goes out of sight. The massive advertisements, rallies, slogans, songs and PR cost a whopping amount of money.

We need to get rid of politicians who have sold their souls to the faces in their mirrors. These are not things that have happened just recently, though they might be appearing in different, and perhaps more ferocious forms now.

The aftermath of the pandemic will demand a far greater consideration of patriotism in our lives than before. Poverty, unemployment and the crisis of COVID victims are going to need tackling while healthcare and the economy will demand attention too.

As I write this afterword, hundreds of thousands of Indians are gasping for breath. The government has failed us. There is no oxygen for those in hospitals, there are no hospitals for those in dire need and there is a state of utter chaos and panic spanning the length and breadth of our country even as the virus rages on fiercely.[288] We have become a laughing stock for the rest of the world. India is being looked at as a third-world country and only pity is coming our way. Almost everybody has lost somebody they have known, loved or were related to.

But in this moment of grief and misery, there is a faint gleam of hope that is rising like a beautiful sunrise at the horizon. The ordinary citizens of India, the most essential depiction of Bharat Mata, have risen to the occasion. We have become each others' saviours when everybody in power seems to have

---

[288]Vikas Pandey, 'Delhi hospitals plead for oxygen as more patients die,' BBC, 2 May 2020, https://www.bbc.com/news/world-asia-india-56940595, accessed 14 June 2021.

failed us. We know that there is only so much we can do when resources are scarce, but we hope that change is on its way and are doing everything we can to ease the pain till then.

The lesson is not just to remember the faces that betrayed us but also to pledge to be each other's protectors forevermore. We need to become us again and reflect on the shared values that make us Indians. Just because we have fallen, we must not let our spirits die. Just because we are angry, we must not lose our national pride. Just because this government has failed us, we must not believe that no government will ever serve us. Just because we are overcome by sorrow, we must not close all doors for light to seep in.

It is a long journey ahead, a life-long mission to reignite the eternal flame of India and then to rebuild our glory by reinstilling hope in our people. Very soon, there will be another narrative built by the propagandists to compel us to overlook the real reasons why we failed so miserably and to trap us once again in the vicious cycle of divide and rule. How we as Indians respond in the aftermath of the pandemic will decide the future of our great nation. Are we going to do what our government tells us to or are we going to make the government do what we the people want it to? Are we going to let the government define what is patriotism or are we going to define it as patriots? Are we going to blindly cheer for populist leaders and their divisive agendas? Or, are we going to do the patriotic thing—our bit for the common good?

We are ending a journey here, but we can begin a new one by asking ourselves what is the common good that we as people, and people as citizens, and citizens as the country, wish to achieve as our shared objective.

Acknowledgements

Vasundhara Baigra, who had the audacity to make a patriot out of a literary critic. This book began as a result of our conversations and her foresight.

Madame Roy, for your love, gentleness and time, your 'serial interviewer' thanks you.

Shashi Tharoor, a patriot to the core, whose commitment to the cause of India is one of the three pillars on which the arguments in this book rest. This book would not have materialized without the many freewheeling interviews over the past seven years.

Romila Thapar, Nayantara Sahgal, Ramachandra Guha, Gyan Prakash, Keki Daruwalla and Vikram Seth, whom I interviewed at various stages, some of which are extracted in this offering.

Manali Das and Saswati Bora, editors who have been a part of this journey.

Mita Kapur, the lady of few words, who provides many of us with the rare virtues of perseverance and humility. A day under her able care is worth more than a year without it in the ink street.

The incredible people at Siyahi, who have been just a click away for this book and more even at the height of the pandemic.

Sanjay, my father, who gave me the life he never had. Sabita, Mother Goddess, whose letters arrived every week without fail for many years, instilling the love for words.

Vidushi, Imtiaz, Anup, Bharat, Vishal, Ashish, Chitvan, Lakshay, Anand, Sourav, Gaurav and Rakesh for always being just a call away.

Chanda, my constant companion and closest ally, for reasons she knows best.

Satyam Rai, Deepak Rani Thapa and Sangeeta Pradhan, teachers of poetry, prose and drama in the most amazing school ever.

Charles G. Mahbert, Jennifer Mahbert and Ajoy Choudhary, who relished and publicized my verses in my teens.

Asha Ramachandran, Usha Mahadevan and Shahid Pervez, editors at *The Statesman*, who taught me to value the ethics of journalism.

Late Keith Flory and R.V. Smith, the veteran journalists who made a difference in every life they touched.

Vishnu Makhijani, Shibi Alex Chandy, Hardev Sanotra, V.S. Chandrasekar and Tarun Basu, former editors at Indo Asian News Service. To them I owe my gratitude for honing my understanding and sharpening my writing.

Kabeer Sharma, Moinuddin Ahmed, Sylvester Tamang, Shweta Senegar and Bobbins Abraham, comrades at *India Times*, thank you.